THE ROMANS IN BRITAIN

THE ROMANS

in Britain

by
R. E. C. BURRELL

illustrated by
TONY DYSON

WHEATON

A Member of the Pergamon Group

A WHEATON REFERENCE BOOK

Other Titles in this Series:

J
913.362
B

First published, 1971
Reprinted with corrections 1972
Printed in Great Britain by A. Wheaton & Co., Exeter

08 016418 8

Contents

PROLOGUE

ONE afternoon in the spring of 1960 a workman employed by the City of Portsmouth Water Authority made the kind of discovery that you quite often read about in the newspapers. He was digging a trench for a water main at the little village of Fishbourne near Chichester in Sussex, when he began to find small pieces of broken pottery turning up as he dug. Farmers have used baked clay piping for draining their fields for at least two hundred years so this kind of discovery is quite common; but these pieces looked different somehow.

The story of how these and other similar pieces led to one of the most impressive Roman finds in Britain is exciting because so many people were involved. It is a wonderful example of co-operation: of amateurs and experts, people who were just interested, others who lived locally and knew the countryside, engineers and citizens, historians and newspapermen—all drawn together by the fascination of seeing the past come to life in a field where animals had been peacefully grazing for hundreds of years.

A lady who lived nearby had noticed several strange things about that field long before the discovery was made. For one thing, the plants growing on that site were different from those in the area round about, no matter what the time of year or the number of animals in the field.

In dry sunny weather she could feel heat coming up from the ground as well as down from above, and when it rained she noticed that a tiny stream running along the edge of the field turned into what she calls "a raging torrent". She also had discussions with the farmer as to why there didn't seem to be any clay in the topsoil although there was plenty elsewhere.

Now that we know what lay beneath the soil it doesn't seem so odd. The clay had been removed for building, and the plants which had colonized the space where it had once been were naturally not the same as those growing on undisturbed land. Furthermore, the heat she felt striking up at her from below was merely the sun's rays reflected back from stone and brick deposits just under the surface. The "raging torrent" was due to the little stream having to carry off the water from the entire area. The Roman drainage system, although it had been buried for centuries, was still apparently channelling water into the stream.

Understandably, this lady watched with special interest when the water company arrived to lay pipes across the field. As she was going away for a short time, she asked those working there to let her know if anything came to light during her absence.

As luck would have it, the engineer in charge and his assistant were sympathetically inclined to this sort of request. He had already been asked by another lady —a professional archaeologist—to inform *her* should anything turn up in the course of his work.

When the mechanical digger began bringing up quantities of red tile, the chief engineer, feeling that there might indeed be something unusual about this site, telephoned the archaeologist and told her what had happened.

She came that same evening, and although it was raining and nearly dark, she made a rough sketch in her notebook with the aid of a torch, and gave her opinion that the tile was Roman. She approached the owner of the land who readily gave permission for further investigation to be made by a team of experts.

The results of a trial trench dug at Easter, 1961 were so exciting that it was decided to launch a full-scale excavation, and for the next few years a large and devoted band of diggers—seven hundred in all—worked under the direction of a University Professor of Archaeology.

Now in many different ways, more and more people were helping in this project. The uncovering and presentation of the remains was a complicated and costly business. The water pipe-line was diverted and the work delayed. Money had to be raised and land to be bought. The local authority even agreed to alter the position of a proposed main road in order to leave the site in peace.

It is obvious from all this that a great many people and organizations were involved; far too many to mention individually. A list of contributors and helpers can be found in the excellent guide book sold in the museum there.

Without all this energy, generosity and enthusiasm there would be nothing at Fishbourne for today's visitors to marvel at. What exactly was all the fuss about? What had the archaeologists found?

At first most people thought that it was a villa, or

Roman country house. These buildings are not terribly rare in this country—over a hundred of them are known in south east England alone—but this one appeared to be of an earlier period than most. And as the dirt and rubbish of centuries was removed excitement rose.

By 1964, it was possible for the leader of the dig to draw up a plan of the "villa". But perhaps this is the wrong word—some experts were thinking in terms of a palace and it is hard to disagree with them. Although part of it still lies beneath the main road and the houses nearby, the plan shows that the building was well over 450 feet (130 metres) square and that it covered about four acres (more than 16,000 square metres)—far larger than any previously known villa.

As the work went on it became clear that the numerous post holes were the remains of the earliest Roman buildings in Britain—probably the granaries and storehouses of the Second Legion at the time of the Claudian conquest. Although Fishbourne is not now on the coast, in those days Chichester Harbour was only a stone's throw away. This then must have been one of the main bases for the invading troops in the year A.D. 43. No wonder the news caused a stir.

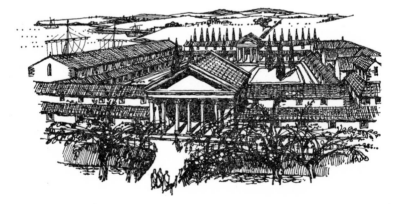

Further work showed that the timber storehouses were probably abandoned by the soldiers as they moved deeper into Britain. Only two or three years after the first landing the granaries were demolished and permanent buildings were begun. By the year A.D. 75 a magnificent palace had been laid out which must have cost a fortune.

Its lucky owner was in all likelihood Cogidubnus, a local king, who was on such friendly terms with the Romans he probably got help from them to build the house as a reward for his military aid during the first few weeks of the conquest.

He must have been a man of immense wealth, for his house contained all the features one associates with the palaces of Roman emperors—baths, colonnades, central heating and decoration on a truly lavish scale—marble, painted wall plaster, mosaic floors and all the rest. A mere description cannot do it justice, it must be seen. So far, only one other such building (uncovered in 1966) is known from Roman Britain. It might have compared with Fishbourne both in size and splendour. It even had its own courtyard garden with a huge ornamental pool, and it was probably the palace of the military governor. Unfortunately, it happens to be just south of Cannon Street in the heart of London, and the demands of commerce in a great city make it unlikely that it will ever be shown to the general public.

At Fishbourne, however, it is easy for the visitor to roam among the ruins (under cover) and imagine the life of a Romanized British court. But if the palace buildings are magnificent there is still another surprise in store.

Just when the diggers thought they had nearly finished, they discovered some regularly shaped discolorations in the area between the wings of the palace. This space was thought to have been a courtyard but now the archaeologists weren't so sure.

If you were to dig a hole in your back garden deep enough to penetrate the surface soil, and then fill it in again, the evidence of where you had dug would remain available almost permanently. Provided that no one disturbs the ground later on, an archaeologist hundreds (or even thousands) of years in the future would be able to tell exactly where the pit was situated and how deep it had been.

To an excavator, differences in soil colour usually mean rubbish pits or post holes for a wooden hut. But surely the owners of a palace would never have had either of these things in the midst of the state apartments? Another two years' hard work with trowel and brush supplied the answer. What they had found were the traces of flower beds! The area in question was not a courtyard at all, but a garden. The marks which had first puzzled the diggers were revealed as places where the royal gardener had cut some shallow trenches and filled them with a soil mixture more likely to encourage the growth of plants.

There had been box hedges and fountains—possibly roses, cypresses and other shrubs, a lawn and several statues. There were even fairly extensive remains of a garden watering system! Not all of the Fishbourne palace has been excavated yet. But enough has been revealed to make it one of the most outstanding Roman discoveries of recent times.

What were the palace builders like? Did they look like us and talk about the same things as we do? What did they eat and drink? How did people in those days get their living? Is Fishbourne completely exceptional —some sort of freak building? (The London palace after all belonged to a high-ranking Roman official.)

What did the people of Britain wear in those days? Did they dress like Romans, or is the old idea of skin-clad, blue-painted, hairy savages nearer the truth? What was Britain like *before* the Romans came? What differences did they make to the way ordinary people lived? Why did the legions come here at all? What were they looking for? How long did they stay and what made them leave?

It is in an attempt to deal with these questions that this book was written. We must start our search for answers by considering what Britain was like in the days before the legions of Claudius Caesar conquered it.

CHAPTER 1

BRITAIN BEFORE THE ROMANS

THE last successful invasion of England was by Duke William and his Normans. It happened in 1066, a date which seems to be fairly well known. There have been three other conquests of this country during the historical period. That is to say, three of which we have any kind of written record. The peoples involved were the Romans, the Saxons and the Danes, but the series of invasions stretches back into the mists of time where history cannot penetrate.

Thousands of centuries before Christ, this land was probably inhabited by only a few hundred hunters and trappers, eking out a bare living in what we call the Old-stone-age. This was a period of almost animal-like existence which lasted, surprisingly enough, more than *five hundred* times as long as all the rest of Man's history put together!

During the ice ages, and in the warm spells in between them, Man learned how to make fire and to chip stones into cutting or shaping tools. He began to drive out wild animals, to occupy their caves himself and to drape their skins round his naked body to keep out the bitter weather. He was developing the art of making himself comfortable in an unfriendly world.

For hundreds of thousands of years he had to be content only with surviving long enough to protect his young children. There was little time for anything but hunting or gathering food. The family was his unit—he could see no sense in any larger group. He fought against other human beings who trespassed in his hunting areas, even killing and possibly eating them as well!

When the ice thawed for the last time, many kinds of "cold weather" animals went with it as it retreated northward. Some of the hunters followed the great herds of mammoth and woolly rhinoceros across what is now the bottom of the North Sea. In those days it was a wide grassy plain but the melting of the glaciers caused a rise in the levels of the world's oceans, and Britain became first a peninsula and then a series of islands.

As the centuries passed, the Channel grew wider, and those seeking a living in Britain had to use small boats to get here. They hunted deer and they fished, even venturing well out to sea when they were after seals and whales. The weather became warmer and there was no need for much in the way of shelter or clothing. We call this period the Middle-stone-age, and before it was over Man had learned new and better ways of doing things.

He invented the bow and arrow, and trained dogs to help him kill his food. He chipped his flints into tiny pieces and used them as borers, scrapers and chisels. He even took sharpened stones and set them in wooden handles to make felling axes and saws. The first crude pottery in Britain was made at about this time.

But in the Near East, Man had discovered how to tame wild animals and grow plants for food. The first farmers arrived here from the continent about 5,000 years ago bringing with them the art of grinding stone tools and weapons to a glassy smoothness. The New-stone-age had begun. For the first time there was no need for Man to wander about looking for food. A farmer simply has to stay in the same place and can therefore own a good deal more than he can carry. Permanent settlements began to develop and the Middle-stone-age hunters were driven off.

Then someone in the Near East found out how to make daggers and spears from bronze. The idea spread slowly, reaching Britain almost two thousand years before Christ. The proud owners of metal weapons lost no time in conquering the flint-using farmers and taking over their lands. Bronze-age men were responsible for such alterations to the skyline as the round burial mounds that speckle our land and the huge circles of shaped boulders, like the one at Stonehenge.

But their bronze weapons were no match for those invaders who were armed with *iron* swords. Bronze-age men were driven away in their turn. If they stayed they were killed or captured, so they retreated to the poorer soils of the north and west. Wave after wave of invaders came here from the mainland, and as the last few pre-Christian centuries trickled away, some of the prehistoric mist starts to blow away. We can say now what the names were of some of the chieftains and the tribes they ruled.

At or about 75 B.C., a group of these fierce, iron-using warriors left their homes in northern France and began to settle in south east England. They were called the Belgae, and were a mixture of German and Celtic races. The mountainous and infertile north west became the hiding place of more refugees from the rich lowlands of the south.

The impression the newcomers had of Britain was very

different from ours. There were no towns, no roads and no bridges. A few areas such as the chalk ridges were bare and windswept, but most of the remainder was covered with thick woods, the haunt of outlaws and wild animals. Even in the south east where cattle were raised and corn was grown, a good deal of what we now call Kent and Sussex was overgrown by almost impassable and trackless forests. The absence of roads made it harder for an enemy to attack their strongholds, and the Belgae were a warlike people.

Raiding their neighbours for cattle and slaves was part of their everyday experience. But sometimes these raids turned into full-scale wars, and the soldiers would fight each other with iron weapons from their light war chariots. Occasionally their kinsmen in northern France and Belgium came across to join in; sometimes it was the other way round.

A few of the chiefs grew rich with plunder and were able to import oil, wine and fine tableware from abroad. Many of these luxury goods were produced within the Roman empire. The Celts of Britain even struck their own coins which were usually copies of Greek or Roman ones. So Britain was already aware of the wealth and power of Rome long before the legions landed in Kent. When Gaul (or France) was added to the Roman dominions halfway through the last century before Christ, British Celts who had crossed the Channel to help their kinsmen gained valuable experience in fighting against the Romans. The general responsible for the conquest of Gaul must also have learned about the Britons and the land from which they came.

The general's name was Julius Caesar.

CHAPTER 2

THE ROMAN EMPIRE AND THE ROMAN ARMY

NO ONE knows for sure how Rome started. Perhaps it was a trading post or a shepherds' market place. But such workaday ideas would not do for later generations of Romans, so they invented a noble ancestry involving Trojan heroes, and they sprinkled their "history" with magic and legend.

There was, however, nothing mythical about their soldiers. In a few decades the legions had succeeded in subduing the whole of Italy. The descendants of the first settlers of the seven hills of Rome had changed their system of government during the course of this conquest. At the beginning, Rome had been ruled by a king but the townsfolk had grown tired of royal families and had thrown them out.

In their place, a council of elders was set up. Its members, or senators as they were called, elected two of their number to rule for one year only at a time. These men were known as consuls, and both of them had to agree on a course of action before anything could be done. With some slight alterations the Senate ran

Rome's affairs for nearly five hundred years. Towards the end of its long life the Senate became feeble, and ambitious men tried to become its master.

The Senate couldn't keep order and there were riots and bloodshed in the streets. To certain types of military men this was a splendid excuse to step in and restore order with their own armies. Some may have fooled themselves into thinking that this was all they were doing. Others were realistic enough to admit (at least to themselves) that what they wanted was power. Power to give everyone orders and see that they were obeyed could only be attained by those who commanded the army. It soon became obvious that whoever was in charge of the army was in fact in charge of the whole Roman Empire. In view of the importance of the army it might be as well to say something about it.

In the beginning—probably during the eighth century before Christ—the shepherds who lived on the seven hills were content just to drive off raiders with whatever weapons they had—enemies in those days must often have found themselves faced by angry farmers waving scythes and pitchforks. Later on the consuls decided to organize the defences properly. Those Romans who could manage to spend weeks away from their farms became part-time citizen-soldiers. Only the rich could afford to do this, so they alone claimed the right to begin a war. When such a decision was made the levy was called up.

The Latin for levy was "legio" from which we get the word "legion". Each legion consisted of men from 17 to 60 years of age, though it was mainly the age groups in between these extremes that saw active service. There were about three to six thousand men in a legion and they were divided up into hundreds or "centuries". Each century had its own centurion—probably a tough, no nonsense, long-serving soldier. Later on in Rome's history, the century was reduced to about eighty men but the words "century" and "centurion" were still used.

As the boundaries of the empire widened, it became impossible for the part-time idea to work effectively. A new kind of professional army came into being composed of men who had signed on for twenty or twenty-five years. The commanding officer of a legion was called a "legate" and his under-officers were known as "tribunes". Apart from the centurions (who had probably risen from the ranks), most of the officers still served on a temporary basis. To obtain any worthwhile job in Rome, a young man had to be able to say that he had been "with the eagles" a certain number of years.

At the beginning of its existence, Rome's soldiers had been lightly armoured and equipped with lance-like spears—rather on the Greek pattern. As time went on the legionary's appearance changed. He wore a leather or metal helmet with side pieces for protection and strips of bronze round the chest and over the shoulders for the same purpose. A neck scarf stopped the rough edges cutting his skin, and under his armour he wore a tunic of the standard Roman pattern.

In warm countries, a pair of stout sandals would complete his uniform, but an extra undershirt or a pair of soft leather breeches might be worn in cold climates. In either case a legionary would have to carry with him his weapons, his engineering tools, his change of clothing, and his food and drink.

The weapons consisted of a dagger, a short sword and a couple of seven-foot (two-metre) javelins. His shield was about fifty by thirty inches (1·25 metres by ·75 metres) and shaped like part of a hollow cylinder. Roman soldiers were expected to lock shields and advance on the enemy, at the same time jabbing him with their two-foot (·6 metre) thrusting swords. The javelins would already have been thrown by the time this stage was reached. Sometimes a group of men would lock their shields together over their heads in order to reach the base of an enemy town wall under cover. The men called it a "testudo" from its fancied resemblance to a tortoise.

Legionaries also built roads and bridges for which special equipment was needed. But because every legion on the march had to erect a proper camp each night, defended with an earth rampart and ditch, a spade and fence-posts were also part of normal luggage!

With personal possessions added on top of all this, the legionaries' loads must have been very heavy. Of course, if it were at all possible, transport was provided for such things. But in the absence of horses, donkeys or mules, a soldier would also have to lug his tent around with him.

The tent was made of leather and was shared by eight men who took turns to erect it and to cook the food. Romans were not spoiled by cookhouses or cafeterias— they not only carted their own grain with them, they also carried grinders and cooking pots.

Having marched all day, perhaps fighting off enemy troops, the legionaries then had to build the camp, including the command area with the officers' quarters, dig a five-foot (1·5 metres) ditch all round it, put up their own tents and prepare their own meals— provided, that is, there were no guard duties for them to do!

Mutiny at these harsh conditions was dealt with by decimation. The commander walked down the ranks touching every tenth man who would be taken away and put to death. Even trivial offences were punished with extra duties or flogging. Sometimes his pay was stopped as well: this was a real hardship to a man who only earned about sixpence a day anyway!

As well as the regular infantrymen, each legion had a number of specialists and odd-job men. There were engineers, doctors, clerks, orderlies, batmen (or servants for the officers), messengers, armourers, blacksmiths, muledrivers and cooks. These are not to be confused with the "auxiliaries", which is what the Romans called their mounted soldiers. They were not usually Italians, and were used on the wings or flanks of the legion to protect the sides and the rear. The Latin word *alae* was used to describe them. At the time of the Republic there were only small detachments of horsemen to each unit of foot soldiers and the legionary tended to think himself superior to his mounted comrade. But towards the end of the Empire, the cavalry played an increasingly important part.

Another important section was the artillery. These were men who were in charge of the spring-loaded war engines which could hurl small boulders, spears and arrows at the enemy. They were designed on the catapult principle and were able to throw stones the size of a football well over half a mile (about a kilometre). When, at a later date, the Roman armies had stopped advancing and were content to defend what they had won, these engines were not used nearly so much, but at the time of the Roman invasion of Britain, the Empire was still expanding.

So that he would know what to do in battle, the ordinary soldier was drilled and force-marched for years on end, until he could almost perform the various manoeuvres in his sleep. Each unit had a standard bearer who held the badge of the unit aloft for all to see, and the commander's orders were relayed by signals blown on huge bronze trumpets.

This constant practice of tactics was the secret of Rome's success. Many of their foes still used prehistoric methods, fighting as individuals, whilst Roman armies fought as one man. A warrior could easily deal with ten enemies one after the other but not perhaps if they all attacked at the same time.

This then was the army as Julius Caesar knew it.

CHAPTER 3

JULIUS CAESAR'S FIRST
XPEDITION—55 B.C.

JULIUS CAESAR had already made himself popular with
ordinary Romans by his conquest of Gaul, which he
began in 58 B.C. It took him three years but he was
hindered by the help given to his Gaulish enemies by
their relations on the other side of the Channel. At the
end of his campaign, Caesar decided to see for himself
what Britain was like.

Many Romans, even well-educated ones, thought that
they knew quite a lot about these islands, but much of
their information was wrong, based as it was on the tales
of wandering traders. Such stories were often spiced
with monsters and unspeakable horrors. Caesar, at least,
knew better. He had fought against the Britons in
France and he must have known that they were no more
uncivilized than most of his other foes.

The Belgae may have been barbarians but they were
not savages. Not everyone walked about naked and
painted blue—not all of the warriors did, and then only
in an actual battle. It is true that they lived in rough
wooden huts but collections of these were as carefully

protected from enemies and wild animals as any Roman town. Traces of the towering earthen walls have actually been found—at Wheathampstead and St. Albans, for instance. The chiefs had their own personal bodyguards and lived in some state, issuing coins and importing luxuries from the Roman world.

Caesar dared not leave the British Belgae alone. They might very possibly try to free Gaul from the Roman legions, which meant keeping a large army on the Channel coast in case they did. Why not use this army to defeat the Britons and remove the danger?

Perhaps the best arguments in favour of the expedition were the plunder, the tribute and the trade which might follow. British tin had been exported to Rome for centuries and the Romans must have known that the Belgae made their swords from the iron sand of the Kent and Sussex Weald. There were also rumours of lead, silver and gold. British wool and wheat, hunting dogs and slaves were well known in Gaul, so a successful expedition would probably pay for itself.

And if Caesar really needed an excuse he had a ready-made one. The Belgic tribes not only fought each other, they often attacked their non-Belgic neighbours as well. From time to time, the latter would appeal to Rome for help. Accordingly, Julius Caesar got together a number of ships and whatever men he could spare from the garrisons of Gaul.

We don't really know what these ships looked like— they were probably not very different from the standard Mediterranean ones, a fact that was later to give trouble. He sailed from Boulogne with two legions of about 5,000 to 6,000 men each. The auxiliary cavalry was to leave from another port a few miles up the coast. There must have been about a hundred vessels all told—warships, supply ships and transports. They were driven mainly by oars, and the journey took about nine or ten hours.

It was an early autumn morning in the year 55 B.C. when the fleet dropped anchor a few hundred yards (metres) from the chalk cliffs of Kent. The cliff-tops bristled with Belgic warriors, some on horses, some in chariots and some on foot. This was obviously no place for a battle, so the anchors were weighed, and the fleet, helped by a slight stern tide, rowed slowly along the coast, the lookouts trying to peer through the Channel haze for a suitable landing place.

Seven or eight miles from where they had first sighted Britain, Caesar decided they must go ashore. All the time the fleet had been drifting with the long slow swell, the Britons had been keeping pace with it. The sun was sucking up the light sea mist and beginning to strike reflections from Roman armour and weapons. The Britons watched the easy dip and slap of the oars warily; they had been compelled to come down from the cliffs so as to be ready for the landing and part of their advantage had gone.

If the historians are right, Walmer beach was the one chosen by Caesar, but it was not quite such a simple proposition as he had imagined. It slopes evenly but at quite a steep angle, and as the transports were rowed in towards the land, their keels bit into the shingle several yards (metres) from the shore.

The grey foam-flecked water eddied and swirled round the hulls; it looked deep and dangerous, and beyond it the Belgae were waiting in ominous lines. The legionaries were hesitant and uncertain until the standard bearer of the tenth legion jumped over the side of his ship. He called to his comrades to follow him as he splashed his way shorewards. There was a moment's silence and then the troops slipped into the sea by the

hundred and started to fight their way to land. The Roman invasion had begun.

Weighed down by their armour and equipment and feeling the treacherous undertow sucking at their legs, they didn't find it easy going. Although a lucky British spear found its mark here and there, that same armour protected them, and most of the two legions eventually got ashore. Once there, they quickly arranged themselves in battle formation and charged.

The Britons, who had held the advantage when the legionaries were struggling through the chest-high waves, had no answer to the organized might of a well-disciplined Roman army. They broke and fled.

But the Romans were unable to follow up these first successes. The ships which should have brought their cavalry over from Gaul had run into head winds and tidal currents. Caesar could have gone ahead, but he felt he must wait until his troops could be protected by horsemen. He gave directions for a camp to be made. The normal marching camp was square with two main roads running through it at right angles and passing out of it through four gateways—one in each side.

When they rolled into their blankets that night, the soldiers probably thought that they had done enough for one day. They had mustered in Gaul the previous evening, loaded their weapons and kit on to the transports, spent a sleepless ten hours on the Channel crossing, fought their way on to a British beach and had then taken some considerable time making a camp and cooking their first meal for more than a day. But they were not to pass very many uninterrupted nights.

Four days later, in the small hours of the morning, before it was even light, a violent and sudden Channel storm blew up. There seems to have been no one on the expedition with any knowledge of local conditions, and Caesar was as surprised as his men to find that the tides were monstrously higher than the three or four feet (metre or so) common in the Mediterranean. The combination of gale and high water was almost fatal; many of the ships were wrecked or badly damaged, and the commander suddenly found himself not only without proper supplies or transport, but virtually cut off from his base in Gaul.

The men were set to work at first light to patch things up. Some were ordered to repair as many ships as possible, while others were sent out to gather the corn which the Belgae had not had time to harvest. The latter, knowing that Caesar was in difficulties, chose that moment to attack the camp. They were driven off but they returned to the fight the next day and for several days afterwards. They were unable to make a hole in the walls of the legionary camp, so they retired to think out their next move.

Had they but known it, Caesar was becoming extremely worried. It had been fairly late in the year when he had left Gaul and this unexpected setback had taken him by surprise. All that the Belgae could think of was that the Romans were here and that they looked like staying. So they sent messengers down to Caesar to ask what he would take to go away. Giving no hint of his difficulties, he demanded hostages and fixed the rate at which they would have to pay tribute to Rome.

As soon as the details had been agreed, the commander packed his men into the patched-up fleet and weighed anchor for Gaul. It was just after midnight when he sailed away, apparently in triumph. He had certainly seen for himself what conditions were like in Britain— he knew for example that the tales of the large corn harvests were true and he had learned that the Belgae were not unbeatable, in spite of their rather odd battle tactics.

But Julius Caesar was a man used to success, and a near disaster such as this must have shaken him. He gave much thought to the problem of transport, and before he left for Rome, he ordered the building of a new fleet, designed to operate in the Channel rather than the Mediterranean. Let the Britons congratulate themselves on his hurried departure. One thing they had overlooked was the Roman habit of never forgiving or forgetting.

Caesar would be back.

CHAPTER 4

JULIUS CAESAR'S SECOND EXPEDITION—54 B.C.

CAESAR came back to Boulogne the following year to find out what progress his new fleet was making. He was pleased to find that nearly six hundred ships were almost ready to be taken over. The shipwrights of Gaul had made them shallower in draught, broader in the beam and with less freeboard. This merely means that the new vessels would be able to get nearer the coast before beaching, and that their cargoes could be unloaded much more conveniently as the decks were a great deal nearer sea level.

This time Caesar wanted to make sure that he had enough men; his new army consisted of five legions instead of the previous two, the whole group being protected by at least two thousand cavalrymen. The ten thousand soldiers of last year's expedition had been barely enough to stave off disaster—Caesar now had more than three times as many men under his command.

The ships weighed anchor on the evening of July 6th, 54 B.C. They sailed and rowed slowly across the thirty miles (fifty kilometres) of the Channel, reaching the Kent

coast towards noon of the following day. There were
no Belgic warriors on the cliffs and the landing was made
without opposition, probably not far from where the
ships had beached the year before.

Swiftly the fighting men lined up in units alongside
their standard bearers, and the stores were unloaded at
the double—Caesar was intent on making full use of the
advantage he had. The legions must have made a brave
sight as their centurions marshalled them into position.
One can imagine the shouted orders, the braying of the
bronze trumpets, the clash of armour and the jingle of
harness as they crunched off over the shingle. The setting sun was beginning to dye breastplate and helmet
an ominous blood red but Caesar was determined to move
forward even though it would soon be dark.

After a night march of a dozen miles (about 20 kilometres) the invaders came to a small river protected by
a hill fort. From Caesar's description, it seems likely
that the river was the Stour, and the place not far from
what is now Canterbury. The Seventh Legion was given
the task of attacking it. This they did by making a ramp
under the cover of their shields and then storming up
it in a frontal assault.

The legions were almost ready to move on again when
for the second time news reached Caesar that his magnificent fleet had been savaged once more by a sudden
storm in the Channel. The superstitious legionaries
might be forgiven for thinking that even the gods of the
Belgae had joined the campaign against them.

Returning to the beaches, Julius Caesar found that
although only about one in twenty of his ships was a
total loss, the number of those severely damaged was too
high for comfort. Working like beavers, the rowers and
the troops managed to pull most of the rest above the
high-water mark, and eventually to repair them. It

seems extraordinary that a military genius like Caesar should make the same mistake twice.

At the end of ten days the work was done and the men were exhausted. The galley slaves could now take it easy but there was no rest for the legions. Caesar mustered his troops and struck inland once more. The Britons had not wasted the breathing space they had been given. Realizing that no tribe could hope to defeat the Romans single-handed, they had joined together under the supreme command of Cassivelaunus, chief of the tribe which lived in the area now occupied by Middlesex, Hertfordshire and parts of Essex.

Cassivelaunus rightly decided that pitched battles were not the best way of dealing with the heavily armed legions, so he sent his foot soldiers home to defend their earth-walled villages, and pinned his faith to his chariots. Julius Caesar wrote a book about his campaigns in Gaul and Britain in which he tells us something of the tactics they used.

Each chariot carried a driver and a warrior. It was a light, two-wheeled affair and highly manoeuvrable. Numbers of them would lie in ambush, concealed in the fringes of the forests. Then they would thunder down-hill, cutting swathes through the enemy ranks. As they galloped, the warriors threw javelins to the right and left of them before dismounting to fight on foot. The drivers took the chariots a little way off so that they could rescue the warriors if things went badly. Against Caesar they usually did go badly. After the surprise of the first attack, the legionaries soon learned to limit their losses, although it was hardly ever possible to launch a counter-attack. They seemed to have treated these charges rather as a postman treats a yapping terrier— with caution but not with undue alarm. At all events, the Belgic charioteers don't seem to have held up Caesar's

advance by very much.   After only a few days he left
the chalk hills of Kent behind and marched down into
the low-lying area surrounding the future site of London.

Of course, London did not exist then. Or if it did, it
could have been no more than a handful of huts on the
banks of the Thames, the river which barred the Roman
advance towards Cassivelaunus's capital.   The Thames
in those days was probably wide and shallow but very
marshy, and the scouts had difficulty in finding a suitable
place to cross.   No one knows for sure where this was,
although several sites have been suggested.

It does seem likely, however, that the legions chose
Brentford in Middlesex.   Some years ago, a lot of sharpened stakes were found embedded in the river mud,
and archaeologists believe that they are evidence of a
Belgic attempt to prevent the crossing.   Other Roman
and Belgic objects have been fished up there from time
to time, and Caesar himself says that the tribes had
prepared underwater defences to hold him on the far

bank. The tribesmen waited for the attack but they were unable to do anything effective. The legionaries and the horsemen swarmed across in an irresistible rush and again the Belgae broke and fled.

Wheathampstead, the capital of Cassivelaunus, was a strongly fortified area of about one hundred acres (40,000 square metres) but it could not hold out against Roman siege tactics. The Romans must have been fed up with the constant annoyance of the chariot attacks, to which they had no real reply. But an earth-walled fortress was the kind of problem they had been trained to deal with. At the end of a short engagement, the legionaries poured over the walls and the tribesmen made off in the other direction.

Now Cassivelaunus was in trouble. Some of his neighbours feared him more than they feared the Romans. They were willing, they told Caesar, to submit to Rome provided that the legions would continue destroying the Belgae. The Trinovantes were the first to do this and a number of other non-Belgic tribes were quick to follow suit.

This was a blow to Cassivelaunus but one which he might reasonably have expected. He had, however, one last card to play. Knowing that the Romans were occupied with Wheathampstead, he staked all on a desperate raid aimed at the Roman base camp in Kent. When it failed, there was nothing left to do but to sue for peace.

There now seemed to be no reason why the legions should not overrun the whole country but Fate again took a hand. The newly conquered territory of Gaul had been almost stripped of soldiers for the British adventure and the Gauls had seized their chance to rise in revolt. The small Roman garrisons would not be able to hold them for very long.

Caesar came to a typically swift decision. He made

Cassivelaunus agree to two conditions—that the Belgic chief should pay tribute to Rome and that he should stop raiding his neighbours. Trying to make sure that these promises were kept, Caesar also claimed a number of hostages. Then he re-embarked his army and sailed away to the continent.

Cassivelaunus had no intention of keeping his word. As soon as the Romans were out of sight, he resumed his raids and wars. The Romans were too busy to interfere. Caesar himself had become more and more involved in politics. Ten years after he had sailed from Britain, he had grown so powerful it appeared that nothing could prevent him becoming the first emperor of the Roman Empire. Shakespeare tells us in his play how those who still hated the idea of kingship plotted to try and stop him. The only solution they could find was to murder him, and civil war broke out once more.

If the news of his death caused the Belgae to rejoice, this was only natural. But the misty islands of the chalk cliffs were not entirely forgotten in Rome during the next century.

CHAPTER 5

THE CONQUEST OF BRITAIN BEGINS

FOR almost a hundred years after Caesar's raids, various generals, dictators and emperors toyed with the idea of adding Britain to the empire. The mad emperor, Caligula, got as far as embarking his troops for the Channel crossing. Then to everyone's surprise he put back to port and ordered the men to collect seashells from the French beaches! However, no other leader had got even this far.

At last Caligula's personal soldiers, the Praetorian Guard, could put up with their mad master no longer. They murdered him and then looked around for his successor. They found Caligula's uncle, Claudius, hiding in the palace in a state of near collapse. The late emperor had ordered the execution of so many people purely for his own amusement, that Claudius had been compelled to act the part of a half-wit for his own protection.

The Praetorians hailed him as emperor, but Claudius had a hard job to live down his reputation as a mumbling, slobbering idiot. It may have been to help him establish himself with the people of Rome that he ordered the invasion of Britain. A successful conquest would win him popularity and respect and perhaps make up for his total lack of military experience. The year chosen was A.D. 43, just 97 years after Julius Caesar had left these shores for the last time.

Claudius's army was to be at least as large as Julius's, so he sent messengers to tell the troops he needed to get ready. There were probably five legions involved—the Rhine frontier forces against the barbarian Teutones provided three of them. They were the Second Legion (Augusta) from Strasbourg, the Fourteenth (Gemina) from Mainz and the Twentieth (Valeria) from Neuss near Cologne. The Ninth Legion (Hispana) had a longer journey—they had been stationed on the Danube frontier in Hungary. The remaining legion was probably the Eighth, and there may well have been detachments of others. The expeditionary force was completed with an equal number of cavalry and other auxiliaries such as slingers, artillerymen, military engineers and so on.

About midsummer of the year A.D. 43, this army of 40–50,000 men had assembled on the coast of Gaul. The military commander, Aulus Plautius, was anxious to start, the ships were ready and waiting, but the troops refused to set foot on board. Apparently some of the old demon-filled stories still lingered on among the Romans. A near mutiny was only averted by Narcissus, one of Claudius's lieutenants, who stood on a platform and spoke to them. The men seemed unwilling to fight beyond the bounds of the known world—if they dared to sail westward from Gaul, wouldn't they be running the risk of falling off the edge of the earth? They weren't inclined to listen to an ex-slave addressing them in Latin with an atrocious Greek accent until a legionary shouted out a rude remark and the whole formation dissolved in laughter. At once the mood changed—now they were eager to get on with the invasion. On what little chances do the fates of nations sometimes hang!

Aulus Plautius's spies had told him of a good landing place which most historians agree was Richborough in Kent—a far better choice than the open beaches Julius Caesar had used. The army made an unopposed landing in three divisions and set to work constructing the usual base camp, traces of which can still be seen. The first objective was to break the power of the Belgic tribes. Free from Roman interference for nearly a century, they now covered almost the whole of south east Britain.

The Belgae had found a leader in the person of Caradoc, or Caractacus, as the Romans were to call him. He was beaten in a battle with the Romans near Canterbury but he managed to escape. The Belgae regrouped their forces and made ready to defend the line of the River Medway, a southern tributary of the Thames. If Caractacus was successful, this would effectively bar the raiders' advance into the rest of the country.

A fierce battle took place which lasted two days. Then a detachment of Batavian troops from Holland was detailed to try and cross the river higher up, thus catching the Belgae from the side and rear. Taken by surprise, the warriors retreated from the river's edge and melted away into the dense forests.

Aulus Plautius pushed on and captured the crossings of both the Medway and the Thames. That way lay open to his advance on the chief Belgic "town". Wheathampstead had ceased to be important and the capital of the south east Britons was now at Colchester. The advance, in fact, had been so speedy that Claudius arrived only just in time to lead the final assault. With the emperor at their head, the legions fought a short battle and the capital fell. Several tribes who were enemies of the Belgae hastened to submit just as they had done in Julius Caesar's time. There was to be no opportunity for Belgic revenge on them when the Romans left. They were here to stay. When the time came for them to go, four centuries had passed and the old tribal patterns had been destroyed for ever.

Among the first chieftains to bow to the Roman conqueror was Cogidubnus, king of the Regnenses. Some people think that he was on friendly terms with the Romans even before the invasion started, and that he might have actively helped the Romans to subdue his neighbours. Some weight has recently been given to this theory by the discovery of the magnificent palace at Fishbourne—only a short distance from Chichester, which was Cogidubnus's capital. It is tempting to think that the Romans helped him build it, or even did the whole thing themselves as a reward for his assistance. They must have treated Cogidubnus and his people fairly generously if the remains in the Fishbourne museum are anything to go by. Not so the tribe known as the Iceni, of whom Boudicca (Boadicea) was to become queen. But more of that later.

Oddly enough, it wasn't Camulodunum (Colchester) which Aulus Plautius chose as his central base in southern Britain. It was a little stony hill standing up amid the Thames-side marshes. A spit of gravel on each bank marked the lowest spot where the river could be easily crossed. Local fishermen probably called it "Llyn-Dun", or some such name. We shall, in all probability, never know exactly what the word was—the Romans always Latinized native names. In the first world war, English soldiers, unable to say "Ypres" in the way that Belgians did, mispronounced it as "Wipers". In the same way, "Llyn-Dun" ("The hill by the pool"), became "Londinium", or London, as we should say today.

It might be wondered why the decision to base the legions on Londinium for the time being was made by the commander and not the emperor. But Claudius had stayed in Britain only sixteen days, returning post-haste to Rome to celebrate his triumph. It was obvious that the invasion had been left in capable hands. Aulus Plautius was so well established that nothing could pry him and his armies loose from British soil. It only remained to see how quickly the Romans could take over the rest of the country.

The Ninth Legion headed northwards to the Wash, the Fourteenth and Twentieth took a line in the direction of the Midlands and the Second set out for the west country, with the knowledge that their stores and supplies would be guarded by Cogidubnus's men. Remains of the wooden buildings which housed these supplies have been found at Fishbourne (see page 10).

The names of the legionary commanders are now lost to us—with one exception. The man who led the Second Augustan Legion out of the kingdom of Cogidubnus was Vespasian. He was later to become emperor, and he showed his military worth by the ruthless treatment he dealt out to his enemies. He overran the Isle of Wight and is reported to have stormed a score or more of the Iron-age hill-forts in the south and west of Britain. Included in this list was Maiden Castle, which must have been one of the wonders of this part of the world.

Like so many of the Iron-age forts, it was a huge hill, ringed with numerous banks and ditches. The inhabitants at the time of the Claudian invasion were the Veneti, a tribe skilled in farming, fishing and sailing. They were also famous for the accuracy with which they could use the sling. This was a small piece of soft leather with thongs attached. The slinger held the thongs and put a round stone on the square of leather. He swung

the sling round and round his head, and when he let
go of one thong, the stone would travel faster and farther
than it could be thrown by hand.

When the fort was excavated in modern times, piles
of round sling stones were found ready for action. The
advantage of this type of weapon was that the defenders
could hide in the ditches behind the ramparts while they
picked the stones they wanted. They could even start
the whirling movement whilst still concealed, only show-
ing themselves for the few seconds it took them to aim.
As the range of a sling was greater than that of a javelin,
the enemy could not get near, particularly since they
were forced to attack uphill.

But Vespasian was an experienced soldier who knew
an even better trick. He ordered the siege engines to be
brought up. His auxiliaries immediately began to wheel
the clumsy-looking spring guns close to the foot of the
hill. When they were in position, the task of winding
and loading began. The heavy wooden arms creaked

slowly backward, straining against the twisting strands of hair and gut. At the word of command the triggers were released and a shower of spears, arrows and boulders descended upon the unlucky Veneti.

The presence at the battle of a ballista (which fired iron-tipped spears) was vouched for in a dramatic but rather gruesome manner. During the excavations mentioned above, the war cemetery of the Veneti was discovered. The bodies seemed to have been buried hurriedly, and one skeleton was found with a Roman ballista spear-head actually wedged into his backbone! Lest his ghost be charged with cowardice, it should be noted that the bolt had passed right through his body from the front before coming to rest.

Missiles could be fired by the Romans over greater distances than the defenders' slingstones could reach. The Veneti were bombarded without cease, and there was nothing they could do—the war engines were well out of their range. Under cover of this barrage, the legionaries advanced behind their shields until they were able to swarm across the parapets and use their stabbing swords at close quarters.

By these and other means, Vespasian and his fellow commanders succeeded in conquering a larger part of Britain than even the Belgae had occupied. The conquests of the Belgae had taken more than a century; Roman arms had managed an even greater task in just over three years.

It is probable that Aulus Plautius's tour of duty as commander-in-chief came to an end at about this time. Claudius was busy dealing with domestic problems (he had been married four times!) and difficulties in other parts of the Empire. The new commander, like the old one, was given the power to make decisions on the spot without asking for Rome's permission. His name

was Publius Ostorius Scapula, and he showed by his
actions that he had summed up the situation pretty
quickly. Without the benefit of accurate maps, he had
noticed a geographical fact that many modern English
people don't even know.

If you draw a line from the south side of the Humber
estuary near Lincoln to the south Devonshire coast near
Exeter, you divide England neatly into geographical
regions. The south east was low-lying country with rich
farmland and the greatest number of people; the north
west was not so fertile nor so well populated, and a good
deal of it was mountainous and inaccessible. The line
so drawn actually runs along little ranges of hills for
much of its length. The legions had advanced as far
as this natural boundary after four years of fighting.
Publius ordered them to construct defensive positions
and dig themselves in. A temporary frontier was thus
set up, and the strong points along it were connected
by a road well over two hundred miles (three hundred
kilometres) long, and known today as the Fosse Way.

The first phase of the conquest was at an end.

CHAPTER 6

ROMAN ROADS

THE Fosse Way was not the only highway the Romans made in Britain. The legionaries laid roads as they went, and their speed and thoroughness were remarkable. Granted that they were helped by the forced labour of gangs of groaning Britons, it is still surprising to discover that only four years after the first landing in Kent, the whole of the conquered area had been covered with a complete network of well-made roads. By A.D. 47 there were almost a thousand miles (over 1,500 kilometres) of them.

There is a common belief that the Roman road went from one town to another like an arrow shot from a bow. It is true that they are straighter than modern roads, for they often travel across hills where an engineer of today would go round. They were designed for the rapid movement of troops, and soldiers can easily climb a slope which might defeat even some of our motor vehicles. But the roads only travelled in direct lines when the country over which they passed was flat. If there were difficulties such as hills, streams or marshes, the road was laid out in a series of shallow zig-zags. To understand why this should be so, we must examine the methods they used.

The Roman engineer would sight the proposed direction with the aid of an instrument called the "groma". It had a number of strings, each with a small weight of lead or bronze on the end. The strings were lined up with a pole driven in the ground a hundred yards (metres) or so away. Surveying or ranging poles were probably painted in bands of contrasting colours, as they are today, so they could be seen against any kind of background. A second pole would be driven in on the same line as the first and so on. It was thus fairly easy to establish the route over flat, level ground.

Let us suppose that the engineer in charge had aimed at a pass in a distant range of hills. When the work reached the pass the next sighting would be taken. To continue the road in the same line might lead it straight into a marsh, or over the top of the highest hill for miles around. Whatever else they may have been, the Romans were not stupid. If the engineer had to change direction a few degrees to avoid an obstacle, he could turn back again when that obstacle was behind him.

Should the pass in the hills be some miles ahead, a survey party was sent forward. The idea was to light a fire at the right point and then to pile on leaves and grass so that the smoke could be seen over great distances. It must have been a pleasant break in routine for the weary soldiers chosen. The only snag was the marching they had to do to get there. If you have ever walked through mud or over sharp rocks, you will know how much more difficult it is than when you have a firm, flat surface beneath your feet.

As soon as the correct alignment had been decided, the digging was started. Two parallel ditches were

made, one on each side of the line, and their distance
apart would vary according to the type of work being
carried out. It might be as much as eighty feet (twenty-
four metres) for a main road or as little as fifteen (4·5
metres) for a minor one. The earth was piled in the
space in between the ditches and rammed down. Layers
of harder material were then added one at a time. There
might be bands of chalk, flint or quarried stone, depend-
ing on what was available.

The whole lot was again rammed down and so was
the top dressing, which might be fitted stones like those
on the Appian Way in Italy; it might be gravel, or it
might be slag from the iron furnaces of Sussex. If the
ground was hard and rocky, little was done apart from
smoothing and marking, but should the subsoil prove
to be boggy, something different was needed. The
simplest way was to build on top of a layer of branches,
gorse or heather, but for a more permanent job, wooden
piles were driven in at both sides of the road and the
space filled in with rocks and stones. These methods
were only used, of course, if the marsh was unavoidable.

The Roman word for the mound formed by these layers was "agger". It was often so high that a man standing to one side of it could scarcely see a fellow soldier standing at the other side. The remains of the huge aggers often give away the presence of a Roman road to an observant seeker. The agger was designed to help the rainwater to drain away quickly, as was the curved surface, or camber of the road.

Up-to-date reports on all the roads in the Empire were kept in Rome and in other important centres. They tried to give an account of places, distances and conditions. One such "guide book" is called the "Antonine Itinerary", and it lists fifteen routes in Britain alone. The word "route" is used rather than "road", for the Itinerary does not always recommend the shortest distance. In the early days of the conquest, roads were made and used for military purposes only, but as time went on, increasing numbers of farmers, merchants, craftsmen, officials and business men travelled along their length. The direct way probably went through lonely country—perfectly safe for an army on the march but not a good idea for a fat merchant with a cart full of samples! In any case, most of the towns and settlements were on the "roundabout" route, and those were the places most civilians wanted to visit.

Poor travellers might go on foot, rich ones on horseback, or perhaps both might ride in some sort of vehicle. Fast two-wheeled traps pulled by horses were not uncommon, but the usual method of transporting goods and passengers was the four-wheeled ox cart. Although mules were sometimes employed for haulage and as pack animals, the imperial couriers always rode on the finest horses that could be had.

The emperor Augustus founded the *Cursus Publicus*, which sounds like the Roman equivalent of the G.P.O.

Unfortunately, the public were not allowed to use this service, which was solely for sending dispatches, reports and official documents. Relay stations were set up every few miles (kilometres) where ostlers kept strings of fresh horses. A messenger could thus gallop at full speed from one posting station to the next, so that urgent letters could be sent from one end of Britain to the other in a matter of hours rather than days. After the Romans left, it was to be over thirteen hundred years before their normal journey times were equalled. There were also a number of *mansiones*, or inns, built at intervals of about twenty or thirty miles (thirty or forty kilometres), rather like modern motels or transport drivers' hostels. Alas, they were also for official use only.

As the conquered area settled down, an increasing number of public eating houses and hotels sprang up, which quite often developed into permanent settlements or even small towns. By this time, the responsibility for the upkeep of the roads had most likely passed to the town councils, who also had the task of repairing bridges —where they existed. There are few remains of Roman bridges in Britain, but the visitor to Corbridge can see parts of the pierwork which once probably carried a wooden bridge over the North Tyne in Northumberland, and a recent discovery in Southwark seems to be the main road leading to Roman London Bridge.

Most rivers were crossed by means of a ford, or more rarely by means of a ferry. Fords which were in use at this period can sometimes be detected by the Roman habit of paving the bottom of the river to give travellers a better foothold while they were wading across.

Early milestones were tall and cylindrical; later ones were made of any boulder that was handy. The distances to the nearest main settlements were shown— sometimes carved into the stone, or painted on its surface.

Augustus had a golden milestone erected in Rome's Forum giving the distances of the principal towns of the Empire marked out in Roman miles.

A Roman mile was shorter than the English mile (about a kilometre and a half) and was known as a *mille passus* (thousand paces). It is from the Latin word "mille" that we get the word "mile". It would be surprising if the Romans put up a stone at *every* interval of a thousand paces. They were probably only to be found at junctions and forks, or wherever a traveller might take the wrong turning. There are about sixty Roman milestones known from Britain, which works out at one for every hundred miles (160 kilometres). Many of them must have been destroyed or used for other purposes in the course of time but the total seems to be rather low anyway.

No one knows for sure how many miles (kilometres) of highway and byway the legions built but it must have been a considerable number. Even if we don't count the lanes and tracks leading away from main routes to mines, farms and villas, something like five to six thousand miles (eight to nine thousand kilometres) are left to us. Many of them are covered by modern arterial and trunk roads, so well were the originals sited. London owes its very existence to the unknown traffic engineers of nearly two thousand years ago who decided that it should be the hub of communications in Roman Britain.

CHAPTER 7

ROMAN BRITAIN REACHES ITS GREATEST EXTENT

AFTER a few months of consolidation, the Romans moved forward once again from their temporary frontier on the Fosse Way. Under Publius Ostorius Scapula, they struck at the northern and western parts of what is now England. The sites of the future Wroxeter and Chester were captured as were those of Gloucester and Lincoln.

When the legions were nearing Wales, they found themselves facing a familiar enemy—none other than Caractacus. We last heard of him immediately after the invasion had started. When he was beaten he escaped to the west and prepared to carry on fighting from there. He was a brave and resourceful foe, the veteran of many encounters with the legions. Once more he escaped after a heroic fight against the legions and tried to get Cartimandua, queen of the Brigantes in the north, to agree that she would help him carry on the struggle. Unfortunately the queen had been having trouble with her own rebellious subjects and had been forced to ask the Romans to help her. In order to keep on the right side of Rome, she made him a prisoner and handed him over to Publius in chains.

Publius was not sure what to do with him and eventually decided to pass the problem over to his emperor. Caractacus was taken to Rome—still in chains. He gazed at the granite, marble and limestone of the greatest city in the world and asked quite simply, "If you Romans have such magnificent buildings, why did you come to steal my poor mud hut?" History does not record the answer—perhaps there isn't one.

So the struggle continued—the Romans making armed forays northward into Yorkshire and westward into Wales. The areas they had won gradually became more like the other parts of their Empire. Towns were planned, houses and villas built, and the day-to-day management of south east Britain was taken over by the civil authorities as the tide of battle carried the legions farther to the north and west.

In Rome, Claudius was having more matrimonial trouble. His last wife persuaded him to disinherit his own son and to adopt a child of hers by a previous marriage. As soon as she had got Claudius to agree, she poisoned him. The new emperor's name was Nero. All this happened in the year A.D. 54, and one of the emperor's first acts was to appoint Suetonius Paulinus to the position of military commander in Britain.

Suetonius was determined to advance the Roman frontiers and he began to study ways of achieving his object. Like the Nazis in occupied Europe, he noticed that the leaders of the resistance movement were often the priests. In the normal course of affairs, the Romans were usually willing to let their beaten foes keep their own religions. But the Druids, as these priests were called, would have nothing to do with Rome, preferring to urge their people on to even greater efforts against

the invaders. Suetonius made up his mind to stamp them
out.

They were masters of a religion, the details of which
are mostly lost to us, and they had a priestly "college"
on the island of Mona, or Anglesey, as we should call it.
Suetonius moved his divisions north westward from
Chester and Wroxeter and attacked the north Wales
coast. Swiftly, he manoeuvred his troops across the
Menai Strait and on to the island. The legionaries
carried all before them, burning, destroying and killing.
Scarcely was the onslaught over, when a messenger
arrived at full gallop from the south. Suetonius must
return with his legions at once. The Iceni of East Anglia
were in open revolt and threatening to undo all the
patient work of the last few years.

The Iceni had submitted to Roman rule soon after
the invasion had started, on condition that their chiefs
should continue to lead the tribe. The Romans had
even lent the tribal nobles money to Romanize their part
of Britain. Repayment was not to be asked for until
several years had passed. The present ruler was a
woman called Boudicca, or Boadicea as she is more
commonly known. When she became queen, an unsym-
pathetic official told her that from thenceforward, East
Anglia would be ruled directly from Rome, and that the
loans which Rome had made were now to be called in.

Queen Boudicca had protested to the local commander
whose only response was to have her publicly flogged.
This was too much for the Iceni, who rose as one man
and murdered every Roman in sight. Alarmed messengers rode from Colchester to the nearest military station
at Lincoln and returned with half a legion. Boudicca's
men met them on the way, fought them to a standstill
and massacred them to the last soldier.

Then they stormed on southward in the direction of

Londinium. The future capital of the United Kingdom was even then a thriving settlement of merchants and probably the largest town in the country. Unfortunately for its inhabitants, there was no town wall they could hide behind. When they heard what had happened to Camulodunum (Colchester), an uneasy trickle of refugees began to flee from the wrath to come.

Suetonius must have used the horse relay stations, for he arrived well ahead of his troops. He surveyed the town and its surrounding countryside and came to the conclusion that it could not be defended. Indeed, he himself might be in danger if he remained there with only a handful of soldiers to guard him. So he abandoned both London and St. Albans to their fate and made his way back to the main body of his army.

Those who remained behind in the two doomed towns were shown no mercy when the rebels arrived. They were hunted down like dogs and killed with unspeakable cruelty. After this confused period of looting and butchery, the Iceni and their allies burned both settlements to the ground.

Archaeologists even now occasionally come across traces of this destruction. It is strange to stand in the car park of the St. Albans museum with the knowledge that only a little way beneath your feet is a thickish layer of ash and charcoal.

Boudicca could hardly have imagined that the evidence of her revolt would still be visible nineteen hundred years later—she was too busy wondering what to do next. The beginning of the uprising had been wildly successful; but the Romans and all their supporters must be driven out if her land was to be free. Her immediate aim was a showdown with Suetonius and his legions. The Roman commander was not over-eager for a pitched battle but he had little choice. The end of the summer was near and Boudicca's warriors had destroyed all possible supplies of food. In addition to these worries, he had only about ten thousand men and would probably be outnumbered by something like eight to one.

However, the rebellion had to be crushed, so Suetonius chose his ground with care. We don't know where the two armies met but it was most likely near High Cross in Leicestershire where the main road to the north west (Watling Street) joined the old temporary frontier (Fosse Way).

The Britons were so confident of victory that they had brought their families with them in ox carts, so that their wives and children could watch the slaughter. Overconfidence has lost as many battles as cowardice. Suetonius had placed his infantry in a solid mass at the top of a slope with thick woods at their backs. On each side were the "wings" of mounted auxiliaries.

The tribesmen were much less disciplined than the legionaries and they charged uphill in their chariots in any sort of order—naked, woad-painted and screaming their war cries. The lines of uniformed soldiers hardly moved an eyelid until the first of the Britons was almost upon them. Then a signal blared from the trumpets and the legionaries hurled a swarm of javelins at the oncoming tribesmen. The charge faltered and the Romans threw another fusilade. The air was thick with spears and the slope before them quickly became covered with the dead and dying. The confusion of noise was punctuated by the neighing of frightened horses as they struggled to free themselves from wrecked chariots and tangled harness.

Another trumpet call and the legionaries drew their short stabbing swords and moved forward in triangular formation, driving a wedge into the ranks of the enemy. At the same time, the Roman cavalry spurred out from the main formation to prevent the Iceni spreading away from the Roman spearhead. Some auxiliaries rode boldly on—right round the back of the opposing host to where the ox carts were stationed. The frightened women and children could not stop them killing the oxen so that the carts could not be moved.

Penned in, the Britons could find no answer and no escape. For Boudicca there was no escape either. She managed to get away from the battlefield but when she realized that all hope was gone, she drank poison rather than wait for the Romans to take their revenge.

The revolt was not yet quite over and it continued to flare up in the succeeding weeks. It might have gone on smouldering for far longer than it did. Suetonius could only offer the rebels death if they surrendered— had they not dealt out the same punishment to three of the most important towns of south Britain? The emperor Nero had other ideas, one of which was that dead men pay no taxes. He recalled Suetonius to Rome and appointed Petronius Turpilianus in his place. The new military commander immediately began trying to pacify the enraged Britons. He was helped by the Procurator, or civil governor, of Britain, Gaius Julius Alpinus Classicianus.

Gaius's name was already known to us from documents but his existence received a rather curious confirmation from a site in London. In 1852, the top half of a memorial tombstone was found during alterations to a building in the city. In 1935, repairs to the London Underground railway brought the bottom half to light, and now the inscription could be read. It was a memorial to Gaius, the stones of which are now in the British Museum. A reproduction is let into the wall at Trinity Square where the original was found, upside down in a turret of the Roman city wall. It is a pity that many Britons have never heard of him, for it was Gaius who first protested to Nero about the bloodthirsty way in which Suetonius was treating the Iceni. Gaius's action undoubtedly saved the lives of hundreds, if not thousands of British tribesmen, some of whom might well have been our direct ancestors. Is it too fanciful to suggest that but for this courageous man, a lot of us might never have existed at all?

The country slowly simmered down as the result of the peaceful policies of governors and procurators who followed those mentioned above. But gentle methods would not work on the frontiers of the Empire. The best defence from the still unconquered uplands was attack, so once more the legions moved on towards the north and west.

This was not the same kind of country as that of the south, now being peacefully Romanized. Here were mountain and hill, moorland and fell. The legions continued to conquer with their usual thoroughness—subduing and pacifying before moving on. The army was like an experienced climber on a difficult rock face, who makes sure that three of his limbs have good holds before he moves the fourth. The commanders conquered, built forts, consolidated and then prepared for the next campaign against the barbarian Britons.

From the eastern end of the Fosse Way, the soldiers of Lincoln struck northwards towards the capital of the Brigantes, a troublesome people who lived in Yorkshire. A permanent garrison was set up at York.

The legions advanced from Gloucester to Caerleon-on-Usk on the far side of the River Severn, thus cutting off the Cornish Britons from those in Wales. Similarly, Wales was isolated from Cumbria when the Romans established strongpoints at Chester and Wroxeter, reaching the sea somewhere near the modern city of Liverpool.

Antonine Wall
DAMNONII
VOTADINI
SELGOVAE
NOVANTAE
Hadrian's Wall
Newcastle
Carlisle

AREA OCCUPIED by
about 78 A·D·

BRIGANTES
York
PARISII

AREA OCCUPIED by
about 74 A·D·

AREA OCCUPIED by
47 A·D·

Anglesey
Chester
Lincoln
DECEANGLI
ORDOVICES
CORNOVII
CORITANI
ICENI
Wroxeter
Leicester
TRINOVANTES
DEMETAE
DOBUNNI
Gloucester
CATUVELLAUNI
Wheathampstead
Cirencester
St. Albans
London
Colchester

AREA OCCUPIED in
43 A·D·

SILURES
Bath
ATREBATES
BELGAE
REGNENSES
CANTIACI
Richborough
Walmer
Dover
Lympne
DUMNONII
DUROTRIGES
Exeter
Maiden Castle
Fishbourne
Chichester
Boulogne

FRANCE

THE ROMAN MILITARY
OCCUPATION of BRITAIN

Finally they extended their rule to the whole of northern England. The year was A.D. 78—it had taken them a third of a century to get that far.

In the same year, Vespasian, who had now become emperor, appointed Julius Agricola to be the new military governor of Britain. Vespasian had been one of the legionary commanders in the original Claudian invasion, so you may be sure that he drew on his own experience of the country before making his choice. He told Agricola to take the whole of Britain into the Roman Empire, so the governor began by making sure that the parts of Britain which were already Roman would stay that way. He reconquered north Wales and secured all the country south of a line running from where Newcastle now stands to the future site of Carlisle.

He ordered the building of fortifications along this line so that he would have defences to retire to if his invasion of Scotland should go wrong. The defences were only ditches and banks but they ran the full seventy-mile (112 kilometres) width of the country—Roman thoroughness again!

During the early part of Agricola's campaigns, Vespasian had died, and was succeeded by his eldest son, Titus. The new emperor did not enjoy his high position for very long, for he died in A.D. 81 after a reign of only two years. But in two years of operations, Agricola had managed to occupy most of the Scottish lowlands south of Edinburgh and Glasgow. For the best part of a century the Romans tried to hold this troubled area against the fierce and warlike natives.

Domitian, the younger brother of Titus, now reigned and to begin with Agricola was permitted to carry on his wars in Scotland. Indeed, he ventured still further. A series of Roman camps has been discovered in eastern Scotland, the last of them very near the extreme north of the British Isles and only fifteen miles (twenty-four kilometres) from the Moray Firth.   So much for the widely held idea that the Romans never penetrated much beyond the line of Hadrian's wall.   But Hadrian was still in the future at that moment, and Domitian had no intention of prolonging the legions' stay in Caledonia.   (The Caledonians were a highland tribe and their name is often used to mean the whole of Scotland during Roman times.)

For a while after Agricola's recall to Rome, at least some Roman troops remained there. Agricola himself must have been bitterly disappointed at not being given the chance to add Caledonia to the Empire.   He even had plans to conquer Hibernia (Ireland), which he thought he could do with only one legion and its auxiliaries.   Rome was not to have such an opportunity again.   The Empire was still growing but not as fast as it had once done.   It reached its greatest extent during the reign of Trajan, who died in A.D. 117.

His successor was Hadrian, who thought he ought to strengthen the frontiers rather than mount fresh wars of conquest.   But military frontiers meant very little to the settled south.   By the time of Hadrian, there can't have been many people still alive who could remember what life had been like before the legions came.

CHAPTER 8

TOWNS

ONE of the things about the Romans was their insistence on town life as the only possible existence. The very word "civilized" is closely connected with the Latin for a town, just as civilization and city dwelling were connected in the Roman mind. So it was only natural that they should wish to see it established in Britain.

One way of doing this was to set up "coloniae". A colonia was a city largely inhabited by men who had gained their Roman citizenship after having been discharged from the army. They were usually given land taken from the farms of the defeated enemy, and for this reason they were normally to be found only in areas whose loyalty was in doubt. They would thus form a pattern of Roman life for the barbarians to copy, and serve to remind them of Roman might. Rome had first tried this system in Italy, long before she was a world power. It worked well and there was no reason why they should not go on using it. The city of Cologne in Germany shows by its name that it originated in this way. The four British coloniae were Colchester

(Camulodunum), Gloucester (Glevum), Lincoln (Lindum) and York (Eburacum).

But, of course, not all Romano-British towns began in the same way. Quite often the occupation authorities encouraged local chiefs to rebuild their old tribal capitals on Roman lines. Encouragement might include loans of money, materials and expert advice. Rome was anxious to collect the leading Britons together into groups so that an eye could be kept on them, and the gathering of taxes made easier. Among such towns were Canterbury (Durovernum Cantiacorum), Cirencester (Corinium Dubunnorum) and Chichester (Noviomagus Regnensium). Exeter, Leicester and Winchester also came into this category, a fuller list of which can be found in appendix 1 at the end of this book.

Most of them continued to be towns long after the Romans left but there are some exceptions to this rule. Silchester (Calleva Atrebatum) was abandoned at the end of the occupation and fell into ruins. Today the field shapes preserve the outline of the town, the actual walls of which can still be seen in many places. In a dry summer, faint, ghostly images of the street plan make their appearance in the withered grass. A good deal of the town has been excavated, although not very recently. St. Albans (Verulamium) is sometimes included with these tribal capitals but it may have been a *municipium*, or self-governing town. Many of the "tribal" towns carry a version of their old names in their new ones. Calleva Atrebatum, for instance, means "Calleva of the Atrebates tribe", and Aldborough in Yorkshire was Isurium Brigantium, "Isurium of the Brigantes".

Some places were neither coloniae nor tribal capitals, both of which were wholly or partly artificial in origin. The "natural" towns began as a result of some local need. That is to say, they were ports, or groups of houses

which grew up at a river crossing or a busy road junc-
tion; they might possibly be markets or collecting points
for a mining area. Some, like Bath (Aquae Sulis) or
Buxton (Aquae Arnemetiae), were favourite spots for
both invalids and holiday-makers.

Not all the towns were governed in the same way to
begin with; the coloniae, however, were built *by* Romans
for Romans, and run on Roman lines from the start.
For a while, the heads of friendly tribes were allowed
to carry on much as they had always done. As the
chieftains died, Rome introduced her own methods.
Eventually, all the towns in Roman Britain were largely
managed in the same way.

About one hundred or so of the most important of
the townsfolk were given the right to elect six magistrates, who held office for one year at a time. They
were expected not only to run the city in an orderly,
Roman fashion, but also to pay for certain public buildings and works from their own pockets. They were
rewarded with Roman citizenship if they didn't already
possess it. Citizenship brought many benefits with it
which were well worth having. If you wanted the law
to protect you in any way at all, you had a tremendous
advantage if you were a Roman citizen.

Very little has been said about London because it was
so exceptional. Before the invasion it could have been
no more than a tiny fishing village. If it existed at all
in the time of Claudius, its sole importance must have
been its position, as it was the nearest place to the sea
where the Thames could be safely crossed. Between
London and the estuary it was difficult to see where the
water ended and the land began as the river was bordered
by mud flats and salt marshes nearly all the way down.
Coming up from the coast, a traveller would have to
wait until he reached the future site of the capital before

the river banks were firm enough to stand on. The engineers of the Roman army saw the possibilities of a spit of well-drained gravel on each side of the Thames. They built a bridge across for the main roads from the south to converge upon. On the north bank, these same roads fanned out, thus making Londinium the centre of the road network.

Some idea of the way London grew during the period can be got by comparing its size with a few of the other towns. Silchester was about one hundred acres (400,000 square metres) and Caerwent only forty-four (about 180,000 square metres). But London occupied three hundred and thirty acres (a million and a third square metres)—almost half as big again as Cirencester, the next largest town. Another startling comparison is in the matter of populations. Most Romano-British towns had about one or two thousand inhabitants but London must have had nearer *fifteen* thousand towards the end of its existence as the commercial capital of Roman Britain. It was so extraordinary that it would be better to consider one of the smaller towns if we want to look at a typical example.

Many of the latter were designed so that the two main roads quartered the town and met at right angles in the centre. This was rather like the normal legionary fortress or camp, but the command area at the cross-roads was replaced by the town hall, or basilica, and the market square, or forum.

The forum was an open space flanked on three sides by shops and terraced buildings through which ran the alleys and lanes giving on to the real heart of the town. Besides being a gathering place for stall-holders and the sellers of local produce, it could be used as a parade ground if the need arose. It was also a meeting place for friends, a centre of gossip, a rallying point for

political meetings, and an occasional stage for entertainments, if there were no theatres.

Along the fourth side was the basilica, where official business was done. Here the town council and the magistrates met, lawsuits were heard, taxes collected and public proclamations read out. The inspector of weights and measures had an office here as did the man in charge of the water supply, and many other civil servants.

The average basilica could seat the entire population of the town in its public rooms, even if they all turned up at once! The citizens of Calleva, for example, were much better off in this respect than we are: their town hall was eighty yards (73 metres) long, twenty yards (eighteen metres) high and the same distance across, thus providing each of the eighty private houses in the town with more than two hundred square feet (over sixteen square metres) of floor space apiece. Public baths and theatres were laid out just as generously. It must have been quite startling for the first Britons who lived in these towns—some of them must have wandered round in a daze, mentally comparing the new surroundings with their own primitive little huts.

The magistrates of each town sent one or more of their number to sit in a kind of national parliament. It could do very little, however, beyond passing votes of thanks to retiring officials and deciding where the statue of the emperor was to stand. The men with the real power were all genuine upper-class Roman citizens.

In name, the emperor ruled Britain from his palace in Rome; in practice he appointed a governor to look after all civil and military matters. The governor tried to see that no one part of his province became too powerful. Later emperors decided, from bitter experience, to divide the governor's job up among several officials, in case the governor became too powerful!

In certain troubled periods, it had been known for military governors to march on Rome with all their troops in an attempt to make themselves emperor. Sometimes they succeeded, but whether they did or not, it meant that their province was left unguarded. The townsfolk then had to look after themselves, and from just after about the year 200 onwards, city magistrates began to build permanent defences.

In many cases, the town had spread out beyond the original plan, which meant positioning the walls to include all sorts of irregular shapes. The engineers employed did their best to give the final design the appearance of Roman order, but the shapes drawn on the next page show what a task they had.

Because of the odd outlines, there were often more than the regulation four gateways. The illustration

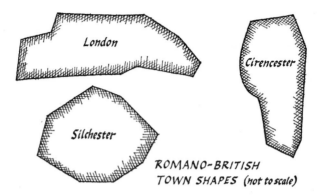

ROMANO-BRITISH
TOWN SHAPES (not to scale)

shows what such a gateway looked like. The walls themselves were commonly a dozen feet (3·5 metres) thick at the base, tapering on the inside to a sentry's walk some twenty feet (6 metres) above the ground. The tops of the gate towers were probably another ten feet (3 metres) above the parapet. Visitors to Lincoln can drive through the Newport Arch, the only Roman city gateway in Britain which is still in use.

The walls were made of concrete faced with local stone. To make sure they did not sag or spread, the Romans laid two or three lines of thin red bricks every few feet (metre or so). There was often a ditch and embankment just beyond the city boundary. Unauthorized visitors would have found it hard to get in, but those with business in the town would have been able to drive or ride straight through the gateway. The entrance road was frequently a double carriageway with one large arch for those coming in and another for those leaving. Sometimes there were small arches for pedestrians on each side of the main road.

There was a guardroom at each gateway, but the sentries were most likely part-time soldier-citizens, not regular legionaries, unless the town happened to be a

military base such as London or York. Once past the
guards, you went along the main street over gravel, or
flat paving stones. Sometimes there were pavements as
we have today, but we should have found the road's
central drainage channel a little strange. Every now
and then you would come across what looked like step-
ping stones. In fact, that is exactly what they were—
the Roman equivalent of zebra crossings, so that people
on foot would not get too wet and muddy in the winter
months. You would pass houses, outbuildings and shops
on your way to the town centre, where the forum was
to be found. As you drew nearer, there were more
public buildings to be seen. You would recognize
temples to various gods, the corporation baths, a theatre
perhaps—and at last you would find yourself in the
forum, gazing up at the basilica.

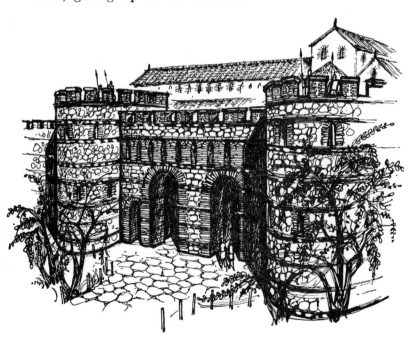

One of the remarkable things was the vast amount of apparently unwanted space within the walls. We have already seen that Silchester had only eighty private houses all told. This means that each house had an average of about four thousand square yards (metres) or more for gardens or outbuildings. With so much space to play with, it follows that the builders restricted themselves to one-storey houses. There is not much evidence that this was so, but it seems natural for the Romanized Britons not to copy the Roman habit of building multi-storeyed apartment blocks. That was all right in the capital itself where land was scarce and conditions were crowded, but in Britain, towns were mostly artificial creations which could be made to whatever size the planners desired.

The majority of private houses were long and narrow with the short end facing on to the street. Each one consisted of a series of rooms side by side with no connecting doors between them. If you wished to go from one room to another you had to go out of the house. For this reason, there was usually a covered verandah running the length of the building. Occasionally the house was also used as a workroom, a shop or both, the owner making and selling things at the place where he lived. The narrow, street-facing end was designed to be opened up for customers during the daytime and heavily shuttered at night. Law and order were maintained by the citizen-soldiers previously mentioned. This can't have been terribly easy, and it was up to the householder to protect his family and property as well as he could—hence the heavy shuttering.

Houses were normally unnumbered and stood in unnamed streets. This must have caused some head scratching among the drivers of carts who were making deliveries —particularly since they were only allowed in the city at night time, on account of the traffic jams! Their task (and that of the military police) was made harder by a complete absence of street lighting.

There was no need in Britain for elaborate aqueducts like those which were used to divert mountain streams into Italian cities such as Rome itself. A wooden, ground-level pipe-line would do the job. It did not have to supply much water, as most houses in Romano-British towns had their own wells. The biggest customer for the public water supply was the municipal baths.

A public bathing establishment was among the first buildings to be erected. The ordinary citizen didn't need to bother about a bathroom of his own. The only private houses to require their own suites of bathrooms were those which lay too far away from the town to make a daily visit possible.

The baths were not intended to be used mainly for swimming as ours are. They were really what we should call Turkish baths. Constantinople became the capital of the eastern Roman Empire, and its bathing customs were adopted by the Turks when they captured it in 1453. So when this particular method of getting clean was brought back into Europe, the label "Turkish" was tied on to it. We ought really to call them "Roman" baths, for that is what they are.

One version consisted of a series of rooms each a little hotter than the previous one with a plunge into cold water to finish off. The price of admission to the public baths was very low but you had to pay extra for such things as the hire of towels or the services of a masseur. You began by undressing in the special room provided and then made your choice. You could work up a damp perspiration as you progressed from room to room, or you could go straight into what the Romans referred to jokingly as the "Spartan". This was a place where an

extremely high temperature was maintained in a dry atmosphere. The nearest modern equivalent is the "Sauna" bath. The bathers were mostly naked but they may have worn loincloths or briefs when they played ball games or did exercises. A miniature leather garment only big enough for a child and shaped like the bottom half of a modern bikini was found on a site at Walbrook, London, and is now in the London Museum.

For the non-Spartans, massage with olive oil on a stone slab was followed by a scrape down with a strigil, an instrument rather like a small, blunt sickle. Both sorts of bathers finished by diving straight into the cold bath. They swam a few strokes before climbing out for a brisk towelling. Very often there were other facilities such as libraries, restaurants, games courts and laundries.

The town of Bath owes its modern name to the springs of mineral-laden water which gush up from underground, and which were used to fill the great baths in the halls above. The remains are well worth visiting, as some of the pools still have water in them, and the largest one is occasionally swum in even now. The Romans called the town "Aquae Sulis", or "The Waters of Sulis", the latter being a local goddess. These same waters were supposed to be even healthier to drink than to swim in. Modern people who tip a couple of teaspoonfuls of health salts from a tin into a glass of water are only carrying on a custom which must have been old even in Roman times. Aquae Sulis had another advantage—the water came up from underground already heated.

Less fortunate places had to warm up the bathwater themselves. The Romans invented a way of doing this which could also be used to provide central heating—not only in public buildings but also in the houses of the wealthy, particularly those houses which were some distance away from towns. Heating was done by means of the "hypocaust" system. The floor of the room to be heated was supported on a number of little brick pillars, thus leaving plenty of hollow spaces under the house. A furnace was lit at one side of the hypocaust and the hot air was drawn through the spaces between the pillars to a flue on the opposite side. After the Romans left, it was to be many centuries before underfloor (or any other form of central heating!) warmth became common once again.

The flue bricks were made of reddish brown clay, as were the roof tiles which surmounted most Romano-

British buildings, even the temples. The temple remains which have come to light in Britain so far cannot compare with the large ornate structures which were erected in Italy and other parts of the Roman Empire. For the most part they are little more than shrines, small and squarish in shape. There are, however, foundations and fragments of larger stone columns at various sites which seem to suggest that the larger, classical kind of temple was constructed occasionally—for example, at Colchester and Bath.

Most buildings in a Romano-British town stood on stone foundation walls only a few feet (metre or so) in height. The main part of the work was carried out in plaster panelling set in wooden frames. All of the interior was plastered to a smooth finish as many of our homes are. Instead of using wallpaper, they painted directly on to the plastered surface. Small fragments of such paintings are nearly all that remain on most British sites, but exceptions are to be found in museums such as the one at St. Albans, where the painstaking work of modern archaeologists has once more restored whole wall panels to the light of day. A larger selection of complete specimens is to be seen in Italian towns like Pompeii and Herculaneum.

One way in which things were done quite differently in Britain was in the matter of windows. In Italy, the houses of the wealthy had square holes in those walls which opened on to the central courtyard. Wooden shutters were the only way of closing them at night. In the tall apartment blocks of the poor, conditions were so crowded that many families had flats facing directly into the glaring sunlight. If you wanted to keep the sun out you could only close the shutters. The trouble with this was that the room was then plunged into darkness.

In Britain, the Romans found that they had to put up

with the rain more than the heat of the sun, so a certain amount of window glass was used in private houses, although the shops still had to use the shutter system. There was no way in those days to produce the clear, display-case type of glass. Even if they could do this, they were ignorant of the art of making it up into large sheets. In all probability, the material used for house windows was thick, bluish-green and almost impossible to see through. It let in the light and kept out the cold and damp, which is all that could be expected.

The British window was most likely a better answer to the problems of ventilation and weather proofing than the Roman shutter. But when we come to consider the last type of public building—the theatre—we are forced to conclude that Romano-British theatres were only a shadow of the mighty structures which stood in Rome itself and elsewhere throughout the Empire. But even if they were smaller than those of Rome, they were tremendous compared with anything that had gone before. They will be more fully dealt with in chapter 12. Suffice it to say here that they were able (like the basilicas) to seat the entire population of the town at once.

Who paid for all this magnificence? Painstaking work by historians and archaeologists has answered the question. It seems that towns in Roman Britain were maintained at the expense of the countryside. The farmers and peasants did not make very much use of the town. It is true that most towns held a weekly market in the forum, where surplus farm produce could be sold. But a good many peasants grew only enough food for their own needs. To pay taxes to Rome they had to work harder and had nothing left over to sell.

The way men farmed will be outlined in the next chapter.

CHAPTER 9

FARMING

WE HAVE seen why the conquerors were so anxious to get town life going and we may be sure that every encouragement was given to the wealthier Britons to move from their earth-walled slums of haphazard mud huts into a well-laid-out city. Most of the people who might rebel would then be gathered together in a place where they could be watched, and tax-collecting would be that much simpler. But this only took care of the tribal chiefs and their hangers-on. What about the rest of the Britons who had always had a grim struggle to exist at all on what they could grow?

There were two quite different ways of farming in Britain even before the conquest. After it, there were at least three. The earliest farmers in this country had used the "scratch-and-scatter" method. In this, only the top two or three inches (few centimetres) of the dirt could be turned over with the rough-and-ready tools which they had. For this reason, only the light soils on the chalky uplands could be used.

The harvests were never very good. In a fair year

they might have a little left over to swap for things which they couldn't provide for themselves—salt, possibly, or iron tools and implements. In a bad year they went hungry. Many of them were forced off their land by the waves of Celtic invaders of the last few centuries before Christ, particularly in south east England where the Belgae were firmly established by the time the Romans arrived.

These primitive cultivators who remained lived on what they produced and kept themselves to themselves. Their small huts were well off the beaten track—what use had they for roads anyway? Travelling in such wild country was a dangerous undertaking in those days. There were wolves and other ferocious animals on the prowl—there were also robbers and brigands. Unless the villages were very close to civilization, Roman tax collectors tended to leave them alone. Was it worth risking death to demand a payment which the peasant hadn't even got? So the peasants remained unaware of what was going on. If an emperor was murdered in far-off Rome, the only reaction from the villagers might well have been "Who's he?" on hearing the news.

The Belgae had brought with them a heavy-duty, wheeled plough which could cut deep and turn the soil far better. The Belgae were able to plough the sticky clay at the bottoms of valleys as well as the sparse hilltop soils. The clay was harder to work but gave bigger harvests. The tiny, "pocket-handkerchief" fields gave way to much larger ones where the new plough could be used properly. Now a farmer could grow far more grain than he could eat. So, whilst the older inhabitants went on with their age-old scratching, the Belgic farmer had a surplus to sell *every* year. With the money he could buy luxuries from the Roman continent of Europe.

When the legions overran south east Britain, it was

the large Belgic fields, heavy with waving corn which they saw first. Rome was always looking for new supplies of grain to feed the growing army of unemployed in the capital, so the commanders of the invasion forces would nod approvingly at the farms they passed. Perhaps they might even pause and run a practised hand through the fat ears of corn, and then go on their way, reassured that the decision to invade was the right one.

Belgic farmhouses prospered during the period of peace which followed the conquest, and the owners used their new-found wealth to turn them into some sort of imitation of genuine Roman farmhouses. Modern archaeologists call them "villas", and several hundred are known in Britain. Most villas, however, show no sign of conversion from a previous building, and it seems certain that the majority of Romano-British farmers built their villas where no house had ever stood before. There is so much to say about the villas that they deserve a chapter on their own.

The third type of farming was not really different in the way it was done but in the siting of the farms. The coloniae referred to in chapter 8 were towns in enemy territory which had only just been conquered. Ex-service men were given pieces of land carved out from the towns' surroundings and slaves to help work them.

The proud owners probably lived in town houses and farmed land only a little way outside the walls of the city. Slave labour costs much less than hiring men to do the work, so "slave" farms could sell their produce at lower prices than others could. The ex-centurion turned farmer might grow rich enough in a few years to build himself a villa out in the country as well as the town house he already owned.

Latecomers had to be content with land farther away from the town. It seems that most towns were surrounded by a belt of farmland two or three miles (three to five kilometres) wide. What was grown on the farm would naturally vary according to what type of country it was in. Wheat seems to have been common, particularly in the first few years of the occupation, with lesser amounts of barley and oats. Barley was most likely fed to the farm animals or used for making beer. Other crops which could be sold or used to pay taxes were peas and beans. Various fruits and vegetables such as onions, leeks, celery and carrots were not grown on farms but in orchards and house gardens, or on smallholdings. Flax was sometimes raised for the making of linen but the main activity appears to have been the breeding of animals—more especially towards the end of the occupation.

Among those raised in Roman Britain were cattle (which had always been famous, even in Rome), horses (which had only been introduced to Britain a few centuries before the Romans came) and less important animals such as chickens, geese, sheep, goats, donkeys and pigs. There is some evidence that in later years the humble sheep took pride of place even over the noble horses and cattle.

The sowing of seeds was done by the broadcast method, where a man walked the length of his field, throwing handfuls of seed corn to the right and left of him. A type of harrow was used to cover them up. Weeding was a hand operation; the idea of a machine hoeing between straight rows of plants was not thought of in Britain until the first part of the eighteenth century. There was, however, one machine that may have been used. This was called the "vallus" and was rather like a large, wooden-toothed comb set on the front of a cart which was pushed from the back by an animal. The teeth tore off the ears of wheat and dropped them into the cart as it went along.

It had to be pushed of course, otherwise the ox or donkey would have trodden down the very grain it was supposed to be harvesting.

The commoner way of gathering in the harvest was by sickle or scythe. The straw was used for many purposes—slaves' bedding, animal feed, floor covering, thatching and so on. When the grain had been carted back to the farmhouse it was spread out on the ground and either trodden on by animals which were driven over it, or beaten with flails in order to crack the husks. The whole lot was thrown into the air so that the wind would carry away the lighter husks leaving the grains of wheat behind.

Storage was always a worry, for rats might eat the crop, or damp weather might make it start to sprout or go mouldy. The Roman farmer used a kind of corn drier something like the hypocaust to solve the dampness problem and stacked his wheat on raised platforms if he could afford the money for the buildings.

Milk was also produced, not only from cows but from sheep and goats as well. Dairying in Roman Britain was not nearly on the same vast scale that ours is; the normal drink being beer for the peasants, wine for the masters and water for both of them. Milk was turned into cheese and probably into butter as well. Lard was another useful by-product, and there was a steady demand for skins of all kinds. Shoes, belts, breeches and harnesses for horses all depended on home-grown leather. Some animal hides were exported to the continent—British leather was well known in Gaul even before the conquest. There was nothing to compare with the vineyards of the Mediterranean lands in Britain but there is some evidence that the growing of grapes for winemaking was not entirely unknown.

It may be that the villas and farmhouses of the countryside went on flourishing long after the towns had begun to decay. This was due to economic reasons—villas paid for themselves and the towns did not. But when the North Sea pirates began their attacks in the third and fourth centuries, the villas were unable to withstand them.

They fell into disuse: some were burned down and others just collapsed. In the course of years, weeds grew over the ruins, and the descendants of the invaders forgot their very existence.

a small, sunken area filled with water and just about big enough for the bather to swim three or four strokes or less. But the plunge bath in this instance turned out to be fourteen yards (nearly thirteen metres) long and four yards (three and a half metres) wide—almost big enough for a swimming gala! Perhaps all the tenant farmers paid a fee so that they and their families could use it as well.

Water was carried to wherever it was needed by pipes made of baked clay, lead, stone or wood—elm and oak were popular for this purpose. Rainwater from yards and roofs was used to flush the lavatories which were probably designed to run away into a nearby cesspit or river. The lavatories were usually to be found near the baths, and consisted of a row of wooden seats side by side with a communal gutter running through below.

The heating of bath water and hot rooms was done by hypocaust or furnace. There was a constant risk of fire in a timber-built house, so the bath suite was quite often made entirely of brick or stone, and was nearly always separate from the house.

The method of erecting the walls of a villa varied from area to area—if there was plenty of good stone nearby the workmen would use it right up to roof level, but if not they made a wooden framework standing on low walls of imported stone and filled in the spaces with plaster panels. It is difficult to be certain but most roofs appear to have been constructed rather in the same way that ours are—that is to say, by erecting wooden rafters on the wall tops, nailing laths across the beams and then waterproofing the whole lot. This was done in most cases with red curly tiles of baked clay, but slate and stone were also used. Stables, barns and sheds made do with thatched reeds or straw.

Coal was used as a fuel but only if it cropped up in

the neighbourhood. The Romans knew its value for heating and cooking but they don't seem to have mined it very much, nor exported it to other areas. Wood was therefore used for most purposes, unless a specially high temperature was needed, in which case the wood might be baked to turn it into charcoal first.

The kitchen staff certainly used charcoal, for they probably did more cooking than their opposite numbers did in Rome. Italians then, as now, made do with a good deal of natural food, as their climate is considerably warmer than ours. In Roman Britain, roasts and "fry-ups" must have been more common than they were in Italy.

The shape and design of a frying pan would not be out of place in any modern kitchen—some pans even had collapsible handles (like the ones some of us take camping!). The chef's helper—perhaps one of the younger slaves—would already have got the stove going. It was a large, squarish mass of brick or stone, sometimes with little hollows scooped out of the top surface in roughly the same arrangement as a modern gas or electric cooker. A hollow was filled with charcoal and lit by means of a spark struck from flint and steel on to a piece of dry tinder. A pair of bellows would help to get the fire to the right temperature. The pan was warmed and the cooking could begin. In Roman Britain, as in Italy, a lot of olive oil was used in kitchens but lard was also used and butter was not unknown. The preparations described here were not of course for breakfast—the family didn't sit down to a hearty meal of bacon and eggs as many of us do for our first meal, they probably followed the Italian custom of starting work with no breakfast at all. If they did eat in the early morning, it was no more than a slice of bread left over from yesterday and washed down with a cup of watered wine.

The next (or first) meal would be towards midday—perhaps at 11.30 or at noon. Again it was a light meal, with cold meat, dried fish, salad and bread. Wine would be drunk sparingly at this meal too. Dinner was in the evening, following the end of work and the afternoon bath. The diners started with small dainties such as shellfish, hard-boiled eggs, olives or smoked fish, rather like the hors d'oeuvres of today. Romans and Romanized Britons must have been exceedingly fond of oysters, for great quantities of the shells turn up on almost every site excavated. British oysters from our south east coasts were famous even in Rome. The important part of the meal came next and consisted of several courses, most of them based on different kinds of meat. The last item was a selection of cakes and pastries, fruit or nuts.

A list of the actual things they ate would not look very different from a restaurant menu of today, with one or two notable exceptions. There were, of course, no new world products such as potatoes and tomatoes, and the purely tropical fruits which we take for granted were almost entirely unknown. There were no bananas or pineapples, but ordinary apples were available, as were pears, cherries, plums, damsons, quinces, blackberries and many more. The canning of fruits and vegetables had not yet been invented, so they had to be dried if they were fancied in the "off" season.

Beans and peas were in common use and so were leeks, garlic, onions, carrots, watercress, mushrooms and so on. There isn't much evidence but it seems likely that the Romans made more use of wild food-plants than we do. For meat they ate pork, veal, beef, mutton and the flesh of untamed animals like the deer and the wild pig. Geese, rabbits, hares, chickens or ducks were often served, and so were birds and beasts which do not turn up on our tables as frequently as they did then. Larks' tongues and stuffed dormice were delicacies—perhaps they also tried blackbird pie and roast hedgehog. Spiced and seasoned sausages were a useful standby.

Thoroughly Romanized Britons insisted on the Roman couch at the table—perhaps allowing the women and children to sit on stools or chairs whilst the master and his male guests sprawled at full length, supporting their heads on whichever hand they were not using to feed themselves. Spoons were used for liquids, and knives were only for cutting. Forks were unknown, so food was put into the mouth with the fingers.

Spoons and knives were much more elaborate than ours; handles were often moulded or carved into animal figures. Favourite subjects were dogs, hares and dolphins. There might be an occasional table vessel in bronze or silver if the family could afford it. There were no drinks to compare with our tea and coffee: imported wine was drunk in quantity with every course, and even a tiny child would have his beaker filled with a mixture of wine and water. The table itself was usually made of wood and stood on four short legs. Examples are known of table legs being carved or turned on a lathe from a rather unlikely material—shale. This is a sort of hard, black, brittle substance not unlike coal and one wonders with what patience the carpenters carried out this task. One false stroke and the leg shattered, giving the craftsman all of his work to do over again. There were other small tables dotted about to take the side dishes, or the condiments (which, by the way, were very like ours).

There was not a great deal of furniture in a Roman villa: tables, chairs and stools have already been mentioned, but it should be noted that the stools were of the folding variety much favoured by modern anglers. As

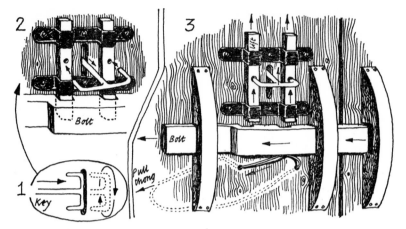

well as quantities of stools, there were lots of cushions scattered about here and there.

Caskets and chests were popular for storage, some of them being fitted with locks. Roman locks were ingenious, but no one ever seems to have invented a lock which would work from both indoors and out. One answer might have been to fit the main door with two separate locks—one for the outside and one for the inside. The most likely form of security at night was a bolt of wood or metal plus a wooden bar across the doors and windows which gave on to the street, or on to the outside world in the case of villas.

As well as chests, other furniture consisted of shelves and cupboards, but the sparseness of bits and pieces was noticeable, particularly in the bedrooms. For sleeping, the family used mattresses spread on raised platforms, with perhaps a chest or cupboard and a stool as the only other permanent objects in the room. All rooms, including the bedrooms, were on the same floor. This was, of course, the ground floor, for although cellars and attics were not unknown in Roman Britain, they seem to have been quite rare. The only stairs in most houses were from one wing to another. Villas were often built on two or three levels owing to the unevenness of the site—it was easier to put in a short flight of two or three stairs than to excavate dozens of cubic yards (metres) of soil.

Statues of gods or goddesses, or family portrait busts were fairly common both in the house and in the garden. The latter was quite likely to be a formal affair with geometrically patterned lawns, hedges and flower beds, rather like the one at Fishbourne. At the moment, Fishbourne palace is the only Roman building in Britain to have had its garden excavated, and the archaeologists intend to cultivate the same varieties of plants which the Romans grew, so that the public can go and see what a Romano-British garden actually looked like.

Most of the interior decoration was reserved for the family rooms and made no use at all of wallpaper, rugs or carpets. Walls were smoothly plastered and then painted with a more or less permanent design. Favourite patterns made use of leaves, birds, beasts and flowers. Alternatively, the artist might produce a landscape or a scene from some ancient myth. The simplest form was a series of panels picked out in colours which were plain, or with a marbled effect, the whole lot being enclosed in surrounds of contrasting colours. Roman wall painting (at least in the provinces) was not terribly well done, and their overall decoration is, to a modern eye, rather harsh and garish. Orange, purple and red turn up often enough in combination to make us think that their colour schemes were somewhat overwhelming!

They had a happier touch when it came to floor covering. This was done with thousands of tiny tesserae, or cubes of various hard materials such as slate, limestone, pottery, tile pieces and so on, known as mosaic. Each material had its own particular hue, so that by arranging them carefully, formal patterns of straight lines and

curves, of pictures of gods, goddesses and heroes could be laid on the floor.

We are fairly sure that there must have been teams of professional mosaic layers going about the country and taking commissions where they could find them. Sometimes an archaeologist is struck by the similarity between two representations of, for example, the four seasons (a firm favourite among villa owners). He can see that the artist had used the same kinds of stone for particular colours and has shown clothing or leaves in exactly the same way.

But some mosaic floor patterns are so crude and badly done, it appears that the master of the house must have ordered his slaves to attempt the work. Perhaps he had already asked a professional tesserae layer to quote him a price for the job and, shocked at the estimate, ordered his slaves to do it instead. Alas, it is only too plain that the slaves were unable to turn their hand easily to this particular skilled occupation.

Top left: *A Roman road, Wheeldale Moor, Yorkshire*
Top right: *Hadrian's Wall near Housesteads Fort*
Bottom: *Portchester Castle, a Saxon Shore fort*

Top: *Roman villa at Chedworth, Gloucestershire, as it is today.* (*The House in the centre contains the site's museum collection*)

Bottom: *Reconstruction of the Chedworth villa*

Top: *Reconstruction of Roman London*

Middle left: *Roman shoes and sandals found in London*

Middle right: *Archaeologists discover the temple of Mithras in London*

Bottom: *A wooden writing tablet and stiluses (pens)*

Top left: (left to right) Roman pins, spoon, probe, spatula and stilus (pen)

Top right: Roman kitchenware—saucepan, ladle, plate and cake tin

Bottom: Remains of Housesteads Fort, Hadrian's Wall

The area to be covered was first cleared and then levelled before the cement foundation was laid, these tasks being left to the apprentices. In the meantime, the master mosaicist would be displaying his pattern book for the family's approval. Even when the final choice had been made, there was still the occasional problem of adapting the proportions to the shape of the floor. It was not always resolved. In one of the largest and best preserved tessellated pavements at Fishbourne, for example, the surrounding border is not quite balanced, and the workmen seem to have made a mess of the design. Three sides of the square have twelve round ornaments each, but the fourth has thirteen! If skilled workmen could make such mistakes, it becomes easier to account for the numerous bad mosaics laid by "do-it-yourself" enthusiasts!

Also at Fishbourne are the earliest Roman mosaics yet known in Britain. They are carried out in black and white and may have served as patterns for other would-be villa owners. The "Four Seasons" theme has already been mentioned; others were Bacchus, Venus and Cupid, water and wood nymphs, boys riding dolphins, or a scene from Rome's mythological history such as Dido and Aeneas or Romulus and Remus.

Unless the mosaic pavement was over a hypocaust, it must have struck cold, particularly in winter. The floors of the less important rooms were often of brick pieces rammed down hard into the bare earth and then rubbed smooth. This was warmer than limestone or marble but perhaps the Roman habit of going barefoot indoors did not apply in Britain. In that case, all those who had to cross an expensive tessellated pavement must have changed their hobnailed boots for some sort of slipper. In fact, soft leather sandals of this type have been found from time to time. There is also some evidence that the womenfolk of the villas knitted woollen socks for the whole family.

No other items of unmistakably Roman clothing made from woven materials have yet been discovered in Britain, but it seems fairly certain that a good many wealthy Britons adopted the Roman tunic and toga. Every member of such families wore at least one tunic, a shapeless, tube-like garment with holes for the head and arms. It was belted at the waist and came down to the knees in the case of children but almost to the ground for an adult wearer.

Only Roman citizens were allowed to wear the toga, which was shaped like a piece cut straight off the edge of a large woollen circle. Many Britons, even those under the Roman influence, continued to make do with a cloak rather than the toga, which had to be wound around the body in a somewhat complicated way.

In Rome, upper-class males were restricted to white. A young boy sometimes wore a red or purple stripe along the border of his toga, but among adults only the magistrates were allowed to do so. As the years of the Empire went by, women began, little by little, to introduce colour into their outfits. A bride had always followed the custom of wearing red and yellow clothing on her wedding day; and black was the sign of mourning then as it is now. But in Britain, it is probable that strict rules about what was good taste (in Roman eyes, at least) were not always kept, and pastel shades for women's dresses, or perhaps even checks in stronger colours for the men were acceptable.

In Italy, underwear seems to have been fairly uncommon, but the climate of these islands must have made the wearing of a loincloth or some form of short pants a necessity. The emperor Augustus is reported to have donned as many as four tunics at once in an attempt to beat the cold. If four tunics were needed in Italy, it may be guessed that some such arrangement was more necessary still in these chillier latitudes. Un-Romanized Britons not only kept their warm woollen cloaks but went on wearing thick baggy trousers under their somewhat shorter tunic-shirts.

The latter grew their hair and beards long as they had always done. Those men who copied Roman fashions in the first century of the Empire were expected to visit the barber often and to shave regularly. As soap was not in general use, and the only sort of razor was a sharpened strip of iron or bronze, this must have been quite painful. Hadrian was the first emperor to sport a beard, and the men of the Empire no doubt followed his example gratefully!

Women's hair styles were more complicated and cannot be generalized about so easily. It may be true to say that they were severe when Rome was young and had become more and more fantastic as the Empire drew towards its close. Women of the early days nearly always parted their locks in the centre, dragging them back to be pinned or tied at the nape of the neck. Then buns became fashionable, and eventually the use of false hair pieces gave rise to elaborate creations of artificial ringlets, curls and waves.

Perfumes and cosmetics gradually came into use in the capital, and there is nothing to say they were not popular in Britain also. In fact many small bottles in glass and pottery from Romano-British sites show that the local ladies were not above copying the latest fashion from Rome. Bronze combs and metal mirrors quite often turn up on villa sites and elsewhere.

If a lady was rich enough to have personal servants, as opposed to mere household slaves, it is most likely that they would have had to attend their mistresses while there was still enough daylight to see what they were doing. The only form of illumination was provided by rushlights, candles and lamps. The Roman lamp was rather like a small, flat earthenware teapot with a wick sticking up from the spout. The bowl was filled with olive oil, and the lamp gave a little light and a greasy smell of burning. Ill-lit houses must have meant that Britons, like the Italian Romans, got up at (or before) sunrise and went to bed early. Unless, of course, there was to be a dinner party that night.

Life in a villa must have been a civilized affair: work came first, but there was plenty of opportunity for sport, rest and relaxation. It was surely the ideal form of existence for those lucky enough to enjoy it. When the Roman administration collapsed some time in the fifth century, and the country was overrun by wandering bands of barbarians, the villa families found it much harder to change their way of life than those Britons who were comparatively unaffected by the occupation.

CHAPTER 11

RELIGION

IT IS unlikely that we shall ever know just how Roman
religion started but it is possible to see how it might have
happened. Men must have realized quite early on that
theirs was a world which they could seldom control.
When a wheat crop is sown, there is no guarantee that
it will be harvested. Floods, hailstones, eruptions, fires
and earthquakes were all signs that men ought not to
become too proud of their ability to earn their own living,
or even to continue living at all.

When disaster struck, early Romans feared that they
had angered a spirit. At first the farmers had only vague
ideas about who or what was responsible for their flooded
fields or their ruined houses. The more superstitious
were quite certain that they alone knew, and they went
on to imagine that these mysterious powers were rather
like human beings. Every field, rock and tree became
the home of a special god or goddess, who had to be
flattered or bribed to bring good luck rather than bad.
Before we laugh too heartily at these quaint notions, we
ought to stop and think how many times we use expres-
sions such as "Mother Nature" and "Old Father

Thames", or how many times we throw a coin in a fountain or refuse to walk under a ladder!

We know the names of some of these early spirits: *Vesta* was a goddess of the hearth, for example, and the *Lares* and *Penates* looked after the fields and the food stores—all very important jobs in a farmer's eyes. But as the Republic grew, these purely Roman spirits came into contact with others.

If you had lived then, you might believe that your local heavenly protector was stronger than your neighbour's. If you could convince him, he might worship yours as well. In some cases, he might even adopt the new god completely and quietly forget all about his own.

By the time the Republic was on the way to becoming a world power, a handful of deities had emerged as "leaders of the league" all over Roman territory. The three most important were Jupiter, Juno and Minerva. Farther down the table were Vulcan, Neptune, Mercury and Apollo. They all sound Roman, and many of them were, but the Romans were quite broadminded about these matters. When legionaries returned from service abroad bringing a new kind of worship back with them, what was the harm? If enough people in Italy were interested, then a new cult was born.

By the time of Christ, the little wayside shrines, caves and rock shelters used by the ancestors of the Romans had given away to much grander establishments. The Greek style of temple building was copied, including the rows of huge columns, the sheltered porches surrounding the inner holy place and the impressive triangular pediments at each end of the roof. The latter were often carved into scenes from Greek and Roman mythology.

There cannot have been many of this type in Roman Britain—possibly not more than three or four, and only in the biggest towns. Although the legionaries adopted

some of the British gods, by regarding them as Roman ones in disguise, they probably continued worshipping them in the old British way.

The remains of a Celtic temple came to light during the last war when work was being done to one of the runways at London Airport. It seems to have been a fairly common kind of church, with a small, square inner sanctuary surrounded by a verandah. The verandah roof was often supported by rows of stone or wooden pillars in the many other examples known.

We must not let the word "church" mislead us. These buildings were not meant to hold the same kind of congregations as their modern counterparts do: they were much too small in any case. A man usually went on his own to the temple and prayed for some favour or gave thanks for a kindness received. It was sheer chance if two or more worshippers were present at the same time. This is not to say that there were *no* larger gatherings. At certain feasts and festivals people would meet together outside the temple in some numbers, and a priest would speak to them or lead them in prayer. So although there were set prayers to be recited on the special days of the god, there cannot have been anything to match the later Christian services. There were no choirs or preachers, nor was there an equivalent of our Holy Bible.

But there was at least one way in which British religions were more like modern ones, and less like those of the Romans. In Rome itself and throughout most of the Empire, certain men served as part-time priests. They either had other duties apart from their priestly ones, or they were elected to their office for one year at a time only. British priests, on the other hand, were professionals. They were called druids and they seem to have been quite important men in tribal life.

They saw to it that worship was done in the proper way, they held ceremonies and generally looked after the religious side of life. They were accused of practising human sacrifice, and attempting to forecast the future by inspecting the victim's internal organs. It was once widely believed that it was on account of this barbarous habit that the Romans decided to stamp them out. But it is much more likely that they signed their own death warrants by urging their warriors to resist the Romans. It is a fact that Suetonius considered the extermination of the druids to be an important part of the conquest.

The gods whom they had served continued to be worshipped without them—very often by the same legionaries who had killed the priests. One of the reasons why the Romans did not try too hard to force Juno, Jupiter and Minerva on the Britons may have been that these old deities were already losing their hold on the mass of the people. They *were* still honoured, even in Britain but they were beginning to lose their monopoly. Their places were being taken by foreign newcomers, whose worship was brought here by soldiers who had served in the Near East.

We know, for instance, that there was a temple in Londinium dedicated to the Egyptian goddess *Isis*. Her name was found on a flask dug up in Southwark. The full inscription was "Londini ad fanum Isidis" ("London, at the temple of Isis"). Serapis, also from Egypt, had his followers, and among the wealthier Romans and Romanized Britons, Mithraism was practised.

The cult of Mithras was probably brought to Britain from Persia by officers of the imperial legions. He was popular too among the well-to-do merchants who thronged the larger cities. Mithras was an embodiment of the sun according to some, and a messenger according to others, playing the part of defence counsel when the time came for Man to be judged by the Gods.

His statues usually show him slaying a bull, a pose something like the pictures of St. George and the dragon which were current during the middle ages. The bull's blood was supposed to have fertilized the soil in the very beginning, and to be the cause of all vegetable life on earth. Temples of this religion remind one of early Christian churches, and indeed, there are some vague resemblances between Mithraism and Christianity. But the differences were still great enough to make the two religions deadly enemies.

Part of the attraction of Mithraism was the "secret society" side of it—some of the initiation rites were childish and at the same time frightening. We don't know a great deal about what went on in the small, dark temples—but perhaps the beginner had to step off a ledge blindfold without knowing where he would land. One fairly certain fact is that the initiate was shut up in a stone coffin, alone and in the dark, to prove that he was worthy of becoming a member.

There were a number of these "mystery" religions, mostly from the eastern half of the Empire, but like the British kinds, they had to take second place to the official state religion.

As the power and influence of the old gods wore away there was more and more disorder in Rome. The Republic came to an end. Augustus was the first of a long line of emperors whose main duty was to see that the largest Empire in the world did not fall apart. At its height the Empire stretched from Scotland to Africa and from Portugal to Russia—a total of about a million square miles (over two and a half million square kilometres). In this huge territory lived a hundred million people—citizens, soldiers, freedmen and slaves. The one thing that kept them together was their common Roman civilization.

The idea of Rome as something more than just a place to live in was carefully nursed by the early rulers. It became the custom to look upon each newly-dead emperor as a god. As such, he was added to the family of heavenly beings, and referred to as "Divine". Before long the worship of dead emperors had spread to living ones, so that the vague feeling of belonging to something greater than yourself had changed into a way of life where citizens were expected to fall down on their knees and to adore the person of the ruler. It was one thing for the army to make its annual vow of loyalty to the Republic, and later on to the emperor—it was quite another when the Caesar in question turned out to be a clown or a monster instead of a god.

It will be remembered that the Iceni had revolted against Roman power early on in the occupation of Britain. There were many reasons for this but one cause was undoubtedly the fact that a temple dedicated to Claudius the god had been built in Colchester. In it,

the tribesmen were required to adore the *statue* of the
emperor, even though he was not present. As if this
were not enough, the Romans insisted that the Iceni
must also pay for the statue themselves.

Not everyone revolted, however. Most people at least
went through the motions of pretending to consider the
emperor divine—but there were two groups who would
not do so at any price. They were the Jews and the
Christians, whose Jehovah had told them to have no
other gods than him, and had expressly forbidden them
to worship idols. To begin with there weren't many of
either group in Rome but their numbers grew steadily
as the years went by. The presence of a large group of
people who wouldn't do what everyone else did was
something the authorities couldn't stand. If they refused
to kneel before the emperor's statue, then they must be
enemies of the state.

It became all too easy to blame the Christians for
every misfortune which occurred, from civil wars and
devastating fires to outbreaks of the plague. Christians
were arrested by the score, by the hundred and by the
thousand. They were executed, often with the most
fiendish cruelty, until the survivors were literally driven
underground. Down in the bowels of the earth beneath
Rome, in a series of subterranean passages known as the
Catacombs, they met and worshipped. They were har-
ried, persecuted and slain for nearly three centuries until
the year 313. The emperor of that time, Constantine
the Great, published the Edict of Toleration at Milan
which allowed them to worship openly. Shortly afterwards, Christianity became the official religion of the
Roman Empire. Apart from one brief period, when the
emperor Julian tried to restore Jupiter, Mars and the
rest to their old status, Christianity never looked back.

No one knows how the religion of Christ came to

Britain but it was probably spread by poorer people. It was particularly attractive to slaves and other downtrodden sections of the community, for it taught that this world's troubles were only a passing shadow, and that the true believer would one day take an honoured place in Heaven. But perhaps its main advantage was that it was open to absolutely anyone. Anyone, that is, who believed in Jesus. Mithraism was one of the many religions which refused to admit females, so it is quite likely that it was the women of Roman Britain who welcomed the new way of life most warmly.

As we have seen, Christians were persecuted throughout most of the Roman occupation of this country. It is therefore not surprising that there is little evidence for their existence. There could be no cathedrals or churches and no magnificent funeral stones: the Romans after all had turned Christianity into a secret society of the less wealthy. Just occasionally, however, the archaeologist's trowel turns up the odd pot or ring bearing the first two letters of Christ's name in Greek, namely the "Chi-Rho monogram" or ⚹ as it was usually shown.

A more intriguing mystery came to light when Roman Cirencester was being excavated. An inscription was found on the wall of a house which reads: "ROTAS OPERA TENET AREPO SATOR". If you rewrite it like this:

R O T A S
O P E R A
T E N E T
A R E P O
S A T O R

you will notice something rather odd. The words can be read, not only in the normal way, but also upwards, downwards and backwards!

This might have been dismissed as the work of a literary doodler with time on his hands—the translation makes very little sense. Word for word, it means: "Arepo, the sower, carefully holds the wheels." But exactly the same magic square has turned up in other parts of the Empire, even in Italy itself. So the inscription must mean something else—but what?

Eventually the code was given a possible solution as a secret Christian password, for the letters can be rearranged in a cross like this:

(A)

P
A
T
E
R
(A)   P A T E R N O S T E R   (O)
O
S
T
E
R

(O)

"Paternoster" is "Our Father" in Latin, the beginning of the Lord's prayer. The A's and the O's left out are supposed to refer to the passage in the Revelation of St. John: "I am Alpha and Omega (A & O), the beginning and the end, the first and the last."

Of course, it's quite possible to make anagrams of the same letters which don't lead to religious codewords.

Even in English they might be rearranged thus: "Or a potter soon repeats a rate." Presumably the same sort of thing could be done in Latin; but if the code solvers are right, it is evidence for the persecution mentioned above.

However, it is from fourth century Britain that most of the clues come. For instance, the plan of a church was recovered from Silchester, and a chapel was found at the Roman villa of Lullingstone. The latter seems to have been a private Christian church whose walls were decorated with praying figures and the largest Chi-Rho monogram yet found in Britain. It was surrounded by a painted floral wreath three feet (a metre) in diameter. It is quite possible that other Christian churches of the fourth and early fifth centuries still await discovery.

During Diocletian's reign, a native of Verulamium who had served seven years with the legions was executed just outside the walls of the town for having given shelter to a Christian priest. This is the only written reference to the persecution of Christ's followers in Britain, and it was not recorded until two centuries after it happened, so the details are rather scarce. We know, however, that his name was Albanus, and he must have been the church's first known martyr in this country. His death was never forgotten, and in the eighth century, a shrine was built over the place of execution.

Eventually a monastery was added and the modern town of St Albans grew up around it, and some distance away from the old Roman city.

St. Alban is said to have died bravely, confident that he would soon be in heaven. No such certain reward could be expected by the followers of other Roman religions. It is true that the earliest Romans had the idea of some kind of life after death but it was a grey, shadowy prospect at best. Those who had done well for Rome were believed to go straight up into the sky, there to become stars or comets. Notions of Heaven and Hell gradually gained ground, probably under the influence of Mithraism and Christianity. Infernus, as the Romans called Hell, seems to have been a dreary place rather than a painful one. Heaven was a never-ending round of dancing and singing in a beautiful countryside setting.

When a man died, his relatives had to make arrangements for the disposal both of his goods and his earthly body. A rich Romano-Briton would probably have left a will, and his heirs would share his wealth according to his instructions. He might also have given orders that some of his slaves were to be set free. A grateful relation might have a tombstone carved with details of the dead man's life.

In the first few decades of the Roman occupation, most dead bodies were laid on pyres of pine branches and burnt—the ashes being put in an urn of glass or pottery before they were buried. Later on, funerals without cremation became customary.

Roman towns were small by our standards and it was considered unhealthy to have cemeteries within the boundaries. Burials took place alongside the roads which radiated out from the gateways. Tombs of all kinds were to be seen—from the plain, ordinary and small, to the decorated, opulent and huge. Coffins which have survived were of stone or lead.

A great deal of information about ordinary people can be got from the memorials erected to the dead—for example, average lengths of lives, names, occupations, nationalities and so on. Numbers of these memorial tablets have been found at York, Chester and alongside Hadrian's Wall. Tombs were regarded by the relations as the homes of the departed in a rather special way, and they decorated the graves with flowers as some of us still do. But Roman mourners went further than this—

they also brought bread and wine to offer. Festivals were set aside on the calendar solely for this purpose.

Not all burials received such loving care. A gruesome discovery was made at Housesteads fort on Hadrian's Wall. Those excavating the nearby civilian settlement found two skeletons, a man's and a woman's. No one could say how the woman had died but the point of a sword had snapped off inside the man's rib cage. The interesting thing was that the two corpses had been buried *inside* the foundations of a house and a new clay floor laid over the top. We don't know how good Roman policemen were at their job, but we may be sure that the murderer could have slept easier in his bed had he known that the evidence of his crime would not come to light for sixteen centuries!

CHAPTER 12

RECREATION

CHILDREN's games which need little or no apparatus have been common for thousands of years. Their origins should be looked for in some early period of history long before the Roman occupation of this country. It is still surprising, however, to find that many street and school-yard games of modern times must have descended from our remote ancestors almost unchanged.

Romano-British youngsters certainly knew all about pastimes such as blindman's buff, hide-and-seek, hop-scotch, pig-a-back, leapfrog and many others. Roman boys bowled hoops and wrestled or swam, whilst their sisters looked after dolls or competed with one another at fivestones.

Dolls have been found with jointed arms and legs, just like those of modern times. Presumably, there were tiny dresses to go with them, although none have yet been discovered in Britain. Smaller children and babies were soothed and distracted by pottery rattles. They were shaped like animals, and their hollow insides contained a number of pebbles. Other toy animals have been

[105

turned up—some of them on wheels, and with a place to tie a piece of string so that they could be pulled along. Carts and chariots—also with revolving wheels—seem to have been popular, as were models of their drivers and miniature pottery soldiers.

Ball games were played which varied with the kind of ball used. A good bouncer can be made by winding woollen thread tightly around a smooth stone. A blown-up pig's bladder or a stitched leather case stuffed with feathers might be the only thing required to start a popular Roman game for three people. The players stood at the points of a large triangle and tried to keep the ball in the air by using any part of the body except the hands. These contests often took place in the exercise yard of the public baths.

Every child was taught to swim, and although there must have been a lot of unofficial diving and ducking during the summer at some nearby river or lake, there doesn't seem to have been anything to compare with our modern national and international galas.

Children had their dogs in those days, and other animals as well. Cats were frequently kept around the house as pets and as mouse catchers. Caged birds were known, and it is certain that mice, hedgehogs, rabbits and hares also occupied a place in quite a few small hearts.

Watchdogs were used then as they are now. More than one notice bearing the words "Cave Canem" ("Beware of the Dog") is known from the Roman world. Stray mongrels could sometimes be a pest. A few roof-tiles are to be seen in our museums with paw prints in them. The workman who had set out his wet clay squares to dry must have been extremely annoyed to find someone's Fido trotting gaily across them. A visible and lasting sign of his annoyance is on display in St. Alban's museum in the form of a tile containing not only the paw print of a dog but also the stone which was thrown at it. The workman's aim was pretty good—his stone landed only an inch or two (a few centimetres) from the footmark.

Romans spent a lot of their lives outdoors—they used the sun as calendar and as clock far more than we do. So it isn't surprising to find that countryside pursuits were very popular, even with town dwellers—when they could afford them.

Romans did more fishing for tomorrow's dinner than we do, but there is evidence that the sporting side of it wasn't overlooked; there are even references to fly fishing for salmon and trout. It was most likely a man's occupation then as it largely is with us: the women were much too busy cooking, cleaning and looking after the babies.

Another nearly all-male sport was hunting. Many kinds of wild animals abounded in Britain then, so you didn't have far to look for your quarry. Among those known to have been hunted were deer, boar, rabbits, hares and bears. Dogs of many breeds were trained to find and kill game, and the chase might be on foot or on horseback. British hunting dogs were so well known outside these islands that many of them were exported. Birds, rabbits and hares were shot with a bow and arrow —spears were used to finish off the larger beasts. Wild-fowlers would lie in wait for ducks and other water birds, using decoys and nets.

In the evening and during bad weather there were indoor pastimes for the whole family. Children could always adapt the games mentioned above, or play "Let's Pretend", but there were other and more formal ways of enjoying oneself.

Squared boards and counters suggest that the Romans had something like our Ludo or Backgammon. To play these two you needed dice, and a number of Roman specimens are still in existence. The pattern of dots is quite often the same as on modern dice. One type of squared board with its pieces resembles the later games of draughts or chess, although this may be just a coincidence.

There were no magazines, radio, television or news-papers to while away an hour or two, so it is tempting to imagine that quizzes and charades may partly have taken their place. There is no definite proof of this, but we know that the Romans did have equivalents of our television drama, current affairs and documentary pro-grammes. These they provided for themselves by means of poetry and play readings, not to mention recitations of historical chronicles or famous speeches.

After-dinner entertainment in a rich man's house might include acrobats, jugglers, singers, musicians and dancers. Music was rarely an art in its own right; its main use was to accompany poetry recitals or singing. There were harp-like, stringed instruments such as the lyre and the cithara, and among the wind instruments, pan pipes were popular. So were tubular whistles; they are known to have been made as long ago as the Old-stone-age, and the Roman version is not much of an improvement on those in fashion thousands of years ago. The tuba and the cornu would be found in a brass or military band if they existed today. The former was a kind of straight trumpet and the latter consisted of a tube almost a dozen feet (well over three metres) long bent into a huge circle.

The bagpipes were played by mountain people in several parts of the Empire, and may at one time have been the latest craze in the capital itself. There is at

least one wind instrument which relied on a reed mouth-piece. This was called the tibia and must have had the nasal and somewhat mournful tone associated with a modern oboe.

The rhythm section of the orchestra could have used almost any two bits of material which would make a noise when banged together. More musical notes were struck from cymbals, drums and tambourines.

Slightly unexpectedly, there was also a kind of organ, worked by air or water pressure. The organist had a keyboard connected to several rows of pipes and even a series of stops with which he could combine different types of sounds.

Musicians didn't just provide performances at evening entertainments in the houses of the well-to-do. They were employed to transmit the army's signals from the commander to the men in time of battle, and as bandsmen with religious processions, or to lend atmosphere to the "games". This is not as strange as it appears, for the games held regularly throughout the year, both in Rome and all over the Empire, had a religious origin. When the Republic won a victory in the early days, part of the celebrations consisted of thanks to the gods and a set of military exercises.

One of the saddest and most regrettable things about these exercises was the slaughter of the prisoners taken in battle. The Etruscans, who were among the first of Rome's enemies, used to force their captives to fight one another until they were all dead. The Romans adopted this custom but it quickly degenerated from a religious observance into human butchery for the amusement of the crowds. Soon, huge arenas, or amphitheatres sprang up all over the Empire. Even in Britain there are examples, although they were on a much smaller scale than those of the Mediterranean areas.

Gladiator fights must have been fairly common in Britain but the slaying of men and wild beasts by the thousand was probably too expensive for the local magistrates who had to foot the bill. Shows involving animals were more likely to be of the circus variety with trainers putting their beasts through a programme of tricks. On the other hand, cock fighting and bear baiting have a long history in this country and may owe their beginnings to the Romans.

Occasionally plays and pageants were performed in the fairly numerous theatres which dotted the country. One of the best of these which is on view to the public is at St. Albans. To be absolutely correct, the establishment at St. Albans is larger than the normal theatre but not big enough for an amphitheatre. The original Greek version was a stage with dressing rooms and scenery bays surrounded by tiers of seats cut into the hillside in the shape of semi-circles. The Romans used this idea for their own theatres, but they also built completely round or oval arenas entirely surrounded by rows of wooden or stone benches rising dozens of feet (twenty or thirty metres) into the air.

The Colosseum in Rome could seat 40,000 spectators in this way, with canvas awnings to protect them from the baking heat of an Italian summer. All these buildings were open to the sky, even in Britain. Audiences here would probably have been glad of some roofing too —but as a protection from the rain rather than the sun. One can imagine the actors from their covered stage trying to shout above the rolls of thunder, whilst the half-drowned spectators huddled miserably in their seats or melted away to the warmth of their own houses.

Native-born Britons were probably more than a little suspicious of playgoing anyway, but they and their Roman masters did have one interest in common—they were both fond of horses. The Circus Maximus in Rome is only one example of a race course for horse-drawn chariots, and similar courses probably existed here too. Lincoln and Colchester have been suggested as possible sites.

Another pastime enjoyed by both Roman and Celt was gambling in all its shapes and forms. Government policy was to discourage it where they could but it was allowed at gladiator and wild-beast fights, as well as on the race track. Wagering on the result of throwing dice was another matter and laws were passed to try and stamp it out. The habit must have been pretty widespread for the Senate to take notice of it. Professional gamblers almost certainly existed, even if illegally. Human nature cannot have changed very much from those days, and it is quite possible that the unsuspecting peasant was robbed of his week's profits by some version of the pea-under-the-thimble trick. A curious pair of dice dating to those days has been discovered which will only roll one total. They must have belonged to one of the underworld characters mentioned above, for the bias was not caused by the wear of centuries but by the fact that each one had been carefully weighted with lead!

CHAPTER 13

EARNING A LIVING

IN EARLIER periods of Man's existence, people made what they wanted themselves or they did without. Civilization gave some men at least the chance to work all day long at a speciality. Even in England's Iron Age there was a little specialization; pottery, for example, was becoming a full-time job. Such products were bought by housewives (if this is the right word!), who were only too pleased to be relieved of that particular chore. This wasn't good enough for the very wealthiest of the Belgae who very often sent their servants shopping in mainland Europe if they could not buy what they wanted at home.

In this way a lot of Roman manufactured objects found their way to Britain even before the conquest. When the legions finally did arrive, the trickle of imports from the continent became a flood. At the beginning of the occupation, nearly all luxury goods were brought over from the Rhineland, France, Spain or Italy. Roman ways of life encouraged the setting up of a large number of small industries, so that more and more high-class goods were actually made in Britain.

Many of these items were made and sold for private profit, although the army often provided for its own needs, and a fair amount of business was carried on by agents of the government in Rome, or on behalf of the emperor himself.

There may have been many reasons for Claudius Caesar's invasion of Britain but it is generally agreed that Rome's main interest was in corn and metals. Mining was one of those industries referred to in the previous paragraph which was almost entirely controlled by the state, so the miner might be regarded as a kind of civil servant. We don't know whether the miners were wage earners or slaves, but in either case, their work must have been hard, dirty and dangerous. It is worth noting that in one or two instances, pit-head baths were provided for them when they came off shift, so perhaps they weren't so badly off.

The Romans were mainly interested in gold, silver, tin, copper and lead. At the moment there is only one known example of a Roman gold mine. It was in Carmarthenshire in Wales, and at least some of the refined gold was turned into jewellery on the spot. Possibly Claudius was misinformed about the presence of gold here. *Irish* gold had been known about in Europe for centuries past—it has even turned up in Bronze Age Mycenae, having been sent to Greece well over five hundred years before Rome was thought of. Caesar's advisers may have thought that the gold from Ireland was mined in England. One thing is certain—no Roman ever made a fortune from English gold.

Silver was a better proposition. It can be got from natural lead by a fairly simple process, although the amount extracted from each lump of lead cannot have been large. There are deposits of lead in North Wales, Derbyshire and the Mendip Hills. It was needed in

quantity for water pipes, coffins, tanks, bath linings and roofs. Large pigs of the metal have been discovered in mainland Europe, each one marked with the imperial stamp.

Copper and tin went into the making of bronze which was always in great demand. Nine parts of copper to one part of tin was the normal formula. If the copper is replaced by lead in a slightly different proportion, a new alloy results which is called pewter. Tin was worked in Cornwall from about the third century onwards, and copper was mined in Anglesey and in North Wales.

Coal was used to smelt many of the metal ores, and it also found its way into the bunkers of private houses. As has already been stated, it was mainly outcrop coal—that is to say, it was only used if it was found lying about on the surface of the ground. There was one exception to this custom: the army dug a number of shallow pits connected by galleries to reach a thin seam of coal in the neighbourhood of Hadrian's Wall. No one knows if the miners were soldiers or civilians. The only definite fact is that there cannot have been any large-scale coal industry as we know it. The use of Somerset coal on the altars of the god Sulis at Bath seems to have surprised most of the Roman writers who mentioned it.

It may come as a slight shock to realize that modern Britain's second most important "digging" industry after coal is the winning of gravel, sand and ballast. Something of the same sort of pattern must have existed in

Roman times. Although metals were important, and rightly so, the quarrying and digging of materials for the building industry cannot have been far behind.

Immense quantities of sandstone, limestone, marble, shale and slate were used, as well as the thousands of tons of gravel liberally scattered over the many miles (kilometres) of Roman roads, both inside and outside the towns. It might be interesting to work out how many thousands of tons of building material went into the construction of a city. In the case of London, the town wall alone must have needed something approaching one hundred thousand tons of Kentish ragstone and mortar.

Roman merchant ships can't have been much different in size from the brown-sailed Thames barges of a later era, so very many voyages must have been made to fetch the stone required from the Medway quarries to London. From time to time, remains of Roman ships are found in the Thames mud: one recent find had part of its cargo still on board; the cargo was Kentish ragstone.

The softer minerals were probably chopped from the quarry face with hammers and wedges. The harder ones needed a special method as the Romans had no explosives for blasting them out. The stone to be worked was heated up by lighting a fierce brushfire against it. When the hot stone was doused with cold water, it split and cracked. After that, the hammers and wedges were set to work in the usual way.

Although much of Britain's mineral wealth was put to everyday uses such as the building of houses and roads, some of it had its place in the luxury trade. Marble panels were often used for their decorative effect, and shale was carved or turned on lathes into such things as rings, furniture legs and bracelets. Thus it was perfectly possible for a Romanized Briton to buy a table made of black Kimmeridge shale encrusted with bronze or silver ornament—all made in Britain.

Talk of buying brings us to money. Even the pre-Roman Iron-age chieftains had not managed without it. Back in the Stone-ages a complicated system of barter was in use, but the arrival of some kind of civilization meant that the more convenient money had to be introduced. The "swapping" of goods was much too awkward to continue. If you need a bronze pot urgently, it's very annoying to find that the only man who has one he no longer wants won't accept anything you have to offer. It's far handier if everyone agrees that certain pieces of metal, shaped and marked in an acceptable way, will have a fixed value. There are still a few examples of British Iron-age coins in existence but they were eventually swept out of use by Roman imperial coinage.

The Roman scheme had a natural order of values running from gold and silver down to copper, bronze and brass. The golden "aureus" was the most valuable piece, weighing about as much as a pre-decimal British penny. Silver coins were favoured by merchants and others for paying bills and similar purposes, but their value varied a good deal.

Sometimes an emperor who found himself short of cash would issue coins with less silver in them and make up the difference with baser metals. The traders passed this on to their customers: if there was only half the amount of silver in the new coins, then they charged twice as much as before. No wonder prices couldn't be kept steady for very long in Roman times!

The less valuable small change was often literally just that—some of the later examples were so tiny that fifty of them could have been completely covered with a pre-decimal halfpenny.

The imperial mints where the money was made (or struck, as it is called) were normally on the European mainland, not in Britain. Now and again, some upstart general in the province of Britannia would seize power, proclaim himself emperor and begin issuing his own currency. It was difficult for the merchants and traders to be sure that such adventurers would last. It was useless to make a fortune in coins that were only valuable just so long as the new "emperor" wasn't defeated. And if the silver had been adulterated with lead, the coins weren't even worth melting down.

Most shopkeepers were craftsmen who lived on the premises and sold their products from the open end of the house. There were exceptions to this rule, particularly in the making of pottery. This was often carried out on a much larger scale, the finished pots thus finding their way over a wider area.

As the demand for luxuries rose, a kind of shiny red-glazed ware from northern Italy was brought in. It is called "Samian" ware, and was very quickly imitated in the mass-production potteries of Gaul. Vast amounts

were imported into Britain, and their broken remains are common on many Roman sites being excavated. This is fortunate for the archaeologist, for although the brilliant red colour and clean lines of these pots remained fairly constant, differences in shape and decoration followed one another so rapidly that it is often possible to date a villa or its extensions from the Samian ware alone.

A few British potters tried to copy the Samian designs by making moulds for the bowls, cups and plates that are hard to tell from the originals. Obviously it would have been far cheaper to make the stuff in Britain than to pay fancy prices for imports. Unfortunately there was no clay suitable in the whole of Britain, so the native craftsmen turned to other patterns.

Among the successful ones were the products of the New Forest area and those of the Nene valley, near Peterborough. The latter region turned out some quite good designs with raised patterns or pictures of animals. This kind of pottery is known as Castor ware.

These were the luxury items but it must not be forgotten that the bulk of all the pottery sold was manufactured by family businesses which had neither the time nor the skilled labour to attempt the high-class article. Many a fortune must have been built up on the making of humbler vessels like the coarse "mortaria". These were mixing bowls which had pieces of grit set into their insides so that they could be used as graters as well.

Money made from trade in this way did no one any good if it were merely stowed away in the Roman equivalent of an old sock. A good many owners of fortunes therefore lent out part of it at interest or used it to finance the building of houses, for example. In this way they became the nearest thing to bankers that Rome ever had. Like modern bankers, they were willing (at a price) to give someone a letter of credit, or an introduction to a "banker" in another town. It might almost be said that Roman merchants were well on the way to inventing the cheque system.

A different industry where the financial help of wealthy men might have played a part was in the manufacture of textiles. Cloth was spun and woven on a fairly large scale, but nothing to compare with our modern factory set-up is known. Maybe some kind of domestic working was the rule. The man with the money would perhaps buy some fleeces from a farmer and then ride round his district sharing it out among his workers who would spin and weave it in their spare time. He would deliver the next lot of wool and collect the finished cloth at the same time, paying the workers for their labour, and then going off to the nearest market town where he could sell the rolls of material and thus make a profit. There is no evidence that this is what happened. It may well be that clothmaking purely for sale was confined to the weaving sheds of large villa estates. But British textiles, particularly cloaks, were well known as far away from Britain as Rome itself and possibly further, so it is quite likely that some kind of organization was set up to satisfy the heavy demand.

There is evidence, however, to suggest that British

weavers included tartan patterns in some of their work. If so, they were carrying on a custom centuries older than the Roman period. The clan tartans of modern Scotland could well be the direct descendants of these traditional designs.

One may imagine the sturdy, brown-sailed merchant ships plying from English ports across the Channel and the North Sea. They carried wine and oil to Britain from Gaul, and sailed back again loaded to the gunwales with corn, cloth, hides and ingots of metal. It is quite possible that pearls were exported from the province. The excellence of British oysters has already been noted in the chapter dealing with the villas: from the vast numbers of shells which are found, it is possible to guess that there must have been a fair number of pearls.

Oyster fishermen lived lonely lives, but perhaps not quite as lonely as the salter. Traces of his craft have been detected round our south eastern shores on the coasts of Essex and Kent. The salter collected sea water in flat clay pans, and used the sun's heat or a fire to evaporate it. The glistening white crystals were scraped out of the pans and packed into pots or bags. The salter and his assistants would then sling panniers over the back of a donkey and load the bags of salt into them. A short journey to the nearest town would net them a small sum of money, but a much longer trip inland would be far more profitable. An even more solitary figure than the salter was the hunter or trapper who supplied the luxury trade in Rome with the skins of seals or bears.

A surprising occupation to find listed is that of millwright. A number of wheels with their gears and grindstones are known—there are museums which actually display parts of them. Sooner or later the thought occurs that if only the Romans had pushed their inventiveness just a little bit harder, they would have become the first technological nation in the world. They had locks and keys, pumps and cranes, complicated mill machinery and even the hydraulically operated organ mentioned previously. It is tempting to ask what they might have done had they been able to make use of a reliable power source, and to apply it to their many machines.

The startling fact is that electricity and the steam engine were both known during the period! A good many Romans must have known all about amber. This is tree gum, fossilized into a hard yellow stone. If you rub a lump of it with a scrap of silk, it becomes slightly magnetic, and will attract bits of dry leaf, paper or straw. The Latin word for amber is "electrum".

The Romans never got beyond regarding electricity as a toy and the same is true of their attitude to steam power. A workable steam engine had been invented by Hero, a Greek living at Alexandria in Egypt, somewhere near the beginning of the Christian era, but it was never developed.

The reason for this astonishing blindness was that the citizens of Rome, like most ancient peoples, were firm believers in slavery. When a man has a house full of slaves to do his bidding, he is unlikely to spend his own time and money perfecting a machine to make *their* work lighter.

We don't know a lot about how the slave system worked in Britain but we do know that it existed. At one time, nearly half the population of Rome were slaves, but very little can be said about how many there were in Britain. There is part of a letter found in London which asks the addressee to sell a slave girl belonging, presumably, to the writer, and there is also a little evidence for slavery from tombstones.

Slave-owning tends to make people lazy and to stop them thinking, particularly if they are engaged in the business of collecting, making, growing or selling. But not all Romans sat about doing nothing (or very little) when slavery freed them from muscle-aching toil. The exceptions were the professional men such as doctors, lawyers, teachers, politicians, administrators and all sorts of civil servants. There is not much proof of their existence in Britain but professional life in the provinces cannot have been very different from that lived in Rome. About the latter we know a fair amount.

The earliest Romans used to cure themselves and their families with herbs—provided that the proper prayers were recited at the same time, of course. Anyone who was particularly good at this kind of thing became accepted by his neighbours as a sort of wise man or witch doctor. But in the thousand years of Rome's history, the art of medicine developed to a surprising degree. There had always been a need for men skilled in the treatment of wounds—at home to begin with and then in the army as Rome's frontiers grew more distant from the city. At no time do military doctors seem to have been very highly thought of, and they weren't given officer ranking as they are in our day. Although the only hospitals so far identified in Britain are in legionary camps and fortresses, it is outside the army that we must look for progress in medicine.

Rome was always willing to learn from any nation which had something to teach. Greek writings on the subject were studied with interest in the capital, and before long, Greek physicians and surgeons began to practise there. Young Romans who showed a liking for this kind of work might be apprenticed to one of the learned foreigners, and in this way methods of curing the sick were learned which were new to Italy.

Roman doctors gradually added to their lists certain vegetable and mineral drugs. They became better at finding out the true cause of a patient's illness and a little less primitive in treating it. The discovery of sets of surgical instruments leaves little doubt that they could perform some operations, even if the bulk of their work was confined to the setting of broken bones. The whole business of cutting, repairing and sewing up has a modern ring, but the unfortunate people operated on were probably fully conscious the entire time. There was therefore no way of carrying out an extended operation, even if the doctor had taken the precaution of making his patient drunk before he started!

Much more like modern times was the bombardment of ordinary citizens with patent medicine advertisements. The commonest of these seems to have been for various forms of eye ointment. We can guess that eye trouble must have been widespread—perhaps as a result of the monotonous porridge diet of the poor.

Equally surprising is the fact that the Romans appear to have had a crude form of the "National Health Ser-

vice" in many parts of the Empire. Doctors appointed by the state to practise in certain towns could be considered civil servants, and as such, they added a little more weight to the huge load of government employees, the cost of which was borne by the man in the street.

Britain, like most other provinces, was run by a governor, or procurator, who not only looked after all aspects of law and order, but was also commander-in-chief of the legions. At a later date, the army and the civilian sides were separated, the military governor from then on having little to do with the day-to-day affairs of the country.

The emperor appointed the civil governor, who then chose a team of men to help him. Some of them were his personal friends, or men to whom he owed favours. But if he had any sense, he would see that his list included real experts who would be able to assist him to make up his mind about any situation which might arise. All of these men were drawn from the upper or middle classes of Rome (at least, to begin with), and they regarded their new jobs as steps in the staircase of their different careers.

Each adviser was supposed to have a deep knowledge of at least one subject. One man would know about tax collection, another about finance, yet another all there was to know on local tribal matters. One important assistant was trained in legal procedures, for the procurator was also chief magistrate with the duty of hearing many lawsuits.

Under each expert there was a small army of clerks, secretaries, writers, interpreters and accountants. Further down the scale still were numerous slaves and freedmen (ex-slaves). They did the humble tasks such as filing the correspondence and writing the kind of standard letter which begins, "Dear Sir, Unless. . . ." They were also able to take dictation from their own head of department, using the normal Roman system of shorthand.

Among the things which concerned the civil servants were recruitment for both the army and the gladiator schools back in Rome, organizing wild animal hunts to supply the amphitheatres, running state industries such as the nationalized farms and mines, seeing to the pay and welfare of the garrison troops, managing the public buildings and supervizing the police force.

Most police activity was a military affair but some retired army N.C.O.'s formed a kind of constabulary for the towns or other places where they were needed. Ex-service men also manned the imperial post office so that important letters and despatches could travel speedily all over the Empire's network of roads.

Under the control of the governor, local town councils saw to the everyday affairs of their own areas. They voted money for public buildings, kept the streets neat and tidy, organized the traders in the market place and generally supervised things. At the start of the occupation, it was an honour for a Briton to be elected magistrate of his native town. One of its rewards was the bestowal of Roman citizenship—a prize worth having in the early days. Only later did he realize that the money for public spending was more and more to come from his own pocket. At last, the drain on the private fortunes of magistrates became so great, that many of them closed their town houses and retired to their villas in the country in order to avoid this expensive "honour"!

It is natural to think of wealthy Britons learning the language of the conquerors, but messages scratched on bricks and tiles show that Latin was spoken and read by quite humble folk. We have no idea what proportion of the people was educated to this standard. Probably it was only the town dwellers. If education in Britain was anything like that in Rome, it was a gruelling business, and a large number of countrymen must have been almost completely untouched by Roman ways of life.

If a Briton did decide to follow the Roman fashion in bringing up his children, he would have had to wait until they were about eight years old before he could send them to school. Until boys and girls had reached that age, they were the responsibility of their mother. At the same time that modern infants transfer to their junior school, Romanized Britons began their formal education. It might be with a tutor at home, or they might have to go to the magister's class in the town forum. Nowhere in the Empire was there anything to compare with the huge schools run by modern governments. The magister was what we should call a primary school teacher, whose job was to thrash the "Three R's" into his unwilling charges. He seldom had more than a dozen pupils, and his classroom was any odd corner of a shop or workroom in the public square. He couldn't afford anything better, for his only earnings were what the parents paid him.

At the age of twelve or so most pupils left school for ever—at least the children of the poor did, particularly if they were girls. The lucky ones went on to a grammarian and stayed with him for about three years. This secondary education was much more concerned with reading and writing than with arithmetic, unless a special course on geometry was requested by the parents. Greek was taught in addition to Latin (rather as today's English children learn French), and the sons of the majority of well-to-do Britons would thus speak fluent Celtic, good Latin and passable Greek. Special attention was paid to fine Greek and Latin literature. Other subjects taught included history and philosophy and (occasionally) music and gymnastics.

The grammarian's aim was to make a boy fluent in reading, writing and above all, in speaking. Positions of power in the Empire went to the good orators. A man couldn't expect to be voted into office if he couldn't put an election address together. Moreover, the presents, the fees and the downright bribes went into the pockets of those lawyers who won their cases, not to the tongue-tied stammerers. A young man might serve an apprenticeship in the courts, or finish off his education with a teacher of Rhetoric who worked at about the same level as a modern university professor.

Considering the number of books a student had to read, it seems strange that the Romans never got around to the idea of printing them. Strange, in that the device of using a fixed set of letters to stamp names on pottery or cakes of ointment was in common use. All books were handwritten on parchment or papyrus. In the days of the Republic, the sheets of paper were stitched end to end and wound on to wooden rollers. The rolls were protected with thin leather covers and stored in racks rather like those used by postmen to sort letters. Quite early on in Empire times, the pages were folded in half and sewn side by side to a backing piece, almost in the same way that our books are bound. A loose wooden cover front and back kept the pages flat: eventually these covers were also fixed on to the backing piece.

The materials used were expensive; papyrus was imported from Egypt, and sheepskin, although produced locally, had to have a lot of work done to it before it was ready for sale. Because of the expense, bound volumes could hardly have been used for school exercises, or other everyday purposes. At the magister's, a different scheme operated. Each pupil carried a pair of hinged wooden boards in his or her satchel. The insides of the boards were coated with softish wax, so that the learner could practise his letters with anything sharp and then rub them out again. An ordinary wooden stick could be used as a pen. It was pointed at one end and flattened at the other. Wooden pens have not survived but there are a number of bone and metal ones in our museums. Similar waxed boards could be used to send letters: some of them show evidence of having been tied firmly together and sealed.

One teacher is known to have saved money by raiding the town rubbish dump for pottery scraps so that his class could write on them at no cost to anyone. The young man making his way in the courts was not expected to jot down his notes on a broken piece of plate—Roman law was difficult enough without that kind of handicap.

Law in the early days of Rome was probably not much more than common sense and tribal custom. As Rome grew, it developed into something much more complicated. Its workings were controlled by the rich and well-born Patricians. The Patricians were the descendants of the original inhabitants, and they tended to favour men of their own class at the expense of the poor people, or Plebeians. The latter fought to change the system, and in the fifth century B.C., the Patricians were forced to make things a little fairer for everybody.

The first changes made were in the actual rules themselves; until then, no one but the wealthy lawyers knew exactly what they were. Twelve bronze tablets, clearly setting out the laws of Rome, were erected in the forum. Just over half a century later, they disappeared during the Gaulish invasions. All we know of them is from fragments quoted by writers living at the same time. Even if the tablets had not vanished, they would have needed revision as fresh problems came up.

The Senate, the various magistrates and the emperors had the power to make such alterations. Most of the early law making that we know about dealt with what are called "civil" cases. Any citizen could take another to court if he felt he had been wronged. Arguments over wills, contracts and boundaries were common, but it is a little disturbing to find that theft or even murder could be settled by the payment of a fine! It must be remembered, however, that Roman law gave very little protection to non-citizens, hence the keenness such men showed to join the privileged band. Serving your emperor as a magistrate or as a soldier carried this reward. Later emperors cheapened the membership by extending the right to become a citizen to almost everybody.

The essentials of Roman law are roughly the same as those of most civilized modern countries. They were that the system should be as fair as possible to all men; that no man should profit unfairly from a law; and that an accused man should have certain rights. These were:

the right to be told what he was charged with, the right
to know what evidence was likely to be given against him
and the right to speak or to call witnesses in his own
defence.

Criminal law, which applied largely to the lower
classes, was usually swift and certain. Criminals were
often denied the rights mentioned above. There was
a tendency among the Patricians to regard a man as a
criminal merely because he had been arrested. Sentences
rarely included spells in prison. An arrested man might
be kept in a military gaol but only while he was waiting,
either for his trial or his punishment. A convicted
criminal was flogged or crucified, very often for what we
should look upon as minor offences. For Roman citizens,
a fine would nearly always settle the matter. If it was
too serious for a fine, the offender could be banished or
forfeit his property. For really serious crimes such as
treason, beheading was prescribed. In practice, the
wealthy were often given the chance to commit suicide,
and thus avoid the disgrace of a public execution.

From all the foregoing, the workaday world of Roman
Britain begins to take shape. It was a world a lot more
"modern" in some respects and nearer to our own ideas
than the centuries which followed its collapse.

CHAPTER 14

THE DEFENCES OF BRITAIN

(i) *HADRIAN'S WALL*

IN THE reign of Trajan, the Roman Empire reached its greatest extent. His death marks the end of the period of conquest. Hadrian, the emperor who followed him, saw it as his duty to hang on to what had been won, and to see that the defences were kept up. He spent much of his reign touring the frontiers, inspecting and advising.

In the year 121, he visited the line of strong points then taking shape between the headwaters of the Rhine and the Danube. Later that same year he came to Britain. According to one of his friends, Hadrian was never content with a one-day ceremonial parade when he descended on a frontier line, and he actually inspected the northern boundary personally. Every yard of it. And on foot! This must have been quite a job, for the line in question ran from the lower reaches of the Tyne to the mouth of the Solway—a distance of well over seventy miles (one hundred kilometres). No wonder his tour round the borders kept him away from Rome for four years.

132

He appointed a new governor when he left Britain, and told him to build a defensive work right across the country. The governor, A. Platorius Nepos, followed the line laid down by his emperor, and the work began in the year 122. The original plan was altered slightly before it was finished but Hadrian's basic idea was at last realized as a superb system of fortifications.

The wall was built in sections by bands of legionaries who were helped by auxiliary troops and even a detachment from the Roman navy. The unskilled labour was probably supplied by the local Britons—unwillingly perhaps, since the wall was to pass right through the middle of their tribal area. Each detachment had charge of about 40-50 yards (35-45 metres) of wall, and when they had completed it, they moved off to another part of the line and began again. The last thing they did was to carve some details about themselves on one of the stones, and in this way we can learn a little about which units were stationed in the north at that time.

The whole system must have taken nearly ten years to build. The actual wall once contained over a million and a half cubic yards (a million cubic metres) of stone, clay and mortar, whilst the two ditches had twice as much material dug out of them. Archaeologists have

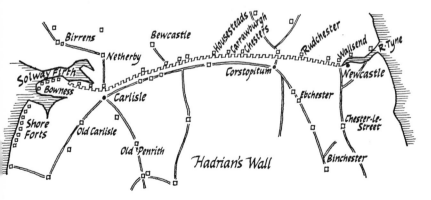

Hadrian's Wall

puzzled over the ditches. Why *two*? A ditch on the far side of the frontier they could understand—it was obviously another obstacle for attackers to get across—but the second ditch lay to the *south* of the wall, and anything up to half a mile (a kilometre) away from it.

The only theory that seems to make sense, is that the nearside ditch (or "vallum", as it is called) was nothing more than the line marking the frontier itself. When the control of British affairs was divided up, the military governor was left in charge of the wall proper, whilst the civil governor's men manned the vallum in order to check passports and collect customs duty. It still seems odd that the two sets of officers needed two separate lines to work from, but perhaps the governors were jealous of each other's powers. After about half a century, the vallum seems to have fallen into disuse.

There was another puzzle for the archaeologists and historians to work on. The wall was eight feet (2.5 metres) thick and probably stood fifteen feet (4.5 metres) high to the sentry's walk. It stretched seventy-three miles (one hundred and seventeen kilometres) across wild, rough country, and was defended by seventeen large forts on or near the wall, each one about a Roman mile (1620 yards (1·5 kilometres) from its neighbours on both sides. There were also two signal towers spaced evenly between the "mile" castles. There were no places for catapults or ballistas, and the forts could only have put up a very thin line of soldiers in time of trouble. If each fort held about two hundred fighting men (there was scarcely room for any more), a quick calculation will show that even if the entire garrison of legionaries, auxiliaries, blacksmiths, cooks, signallers, orderlies and all the other "odds and ends" were to man the wall, a soldier would find that he had only two comrades within twenty yards (twenty metres) of him.

This must mean that the wall was never intended to beat off massive direct attacks but was more like the Berlin wall. In each case there are people on both sides, not only of the same race but of the same family. In both examples, a determined assault must have succeeded. In each instance, the purpose of the wall was merely to control the movement of people who wanted to cross a border. And if the frontier guards were ever taken away from either of these walls, neither of them would have been much of a hindrance to an attack.

In the case of Hadrian's Wall, this happened more than once, and soldiers were actually removed. However, the first time it occurred was a happier occasion for the Romans than any of the later ones were to be. The governor decided that the best way to deal with troublesome tribesmen to the north of the line was to go out and try to beat them in a proper battle.

The legions set out for Scotland in the year 139. They used (and in some cases, rebuilt) the forts left behind by Julius Agricola years before. The troops conquered all of southern Scotland, and their general, Urbicus, built another wall across the narrow part of the country, between where Edinburgh and Glasgow now stand. It is known as the Antonine Wall, after the ruling emperor, Antoninus Pius.

The Antonine Wall is only half the length of Hadrian's and should have been easier to defend. True, it was made of turf and clay rather than stone and mortar, but it was fourteen feet (4·26 metres) wide and twelve feet (3·65 metres) high, being protected by closely set fortlets and a frontal ditch forty feet (12 metres) wide and twelve feet (3·65 metres) deep. While they were at it, the legions tried to make their own task easier by carrying off many of the inhabitants and "press-ganging" them into Roman units serving on the Rhine frontier.

The Antonine Wall between the Forth and Clyde rivers was held, in all probability, for a good deal less than an average lifetime. There was trouble with rebellious tribes in the north of England so the Romans abandoned the turf wall and fell back on their original defence line.

On at least three occasions that we know of, the legions were pulled *back* from Hadrian's Wall, and each time the Caledonian barbarians swept across it. The usual reason for withdrawal of troops was trouble in Rome— there was civil war, or the emperor had been murdered, a not uncommon state of affairs. If the local British commander was an ambitious man he might try to become emperor himself. In the latter days of the Empire, it was nearly always a victorious general who succeeded to the throne—usually the first one who could get to Rome with his troops!

This happened in the year 197. Clodius Albinus, governor of Britannia, quarrelled with the emperor, Severus, and set out for Rome with all his British legions. He was beaten in a battle near Lyons in France and committed suicide. Severus was unable to punish him, and the damage in Britain was already done. The Caledonians soon found out that there was no one on the wall so they crossed it and proceeded to wreck every military work they came upon. Severus, now firmly established as emperor, sent Virius Lupus to clear them out again. Eventually the emperor himself came to Britain with his sons Geta and Caracalla. He won a number of battles against the barbarians, but after three years of hard fighting he died at York in the year 211.

The wall was again overrun in 296 when the two Roman officers, Carausius and Allectus tried to seize power. (See next section.) Once more the damage was repaired but in 367 there seems to have been a very heavy attack on Roman Britain. Barbarians from Scotland and

Ireland were joined by bands of Saxon pirates. This time Theodosius was sent to deal with them and to rebuild the wall.

Only fourteen years later, Magnus Maximus followed the same adventurous path and took his legions off to Rome. The Caledonians poured south yet again, and this time history is silent as to what happened afterwards. All we know is that the year 383 saw the last defence of the northernmost limit of the Empire by regular Roman soldiers. There can't have been many of them left, for Magnus Maximus had taken most of the army units with him. It didn't do him a lot of good. After a few successes, he was defeated by Theodosius, who had now become emperor. He was captured after the battle and beheaded.

What happened to the wall in the years immediately after these events, we don't know. It survived through the ages as a monument to the Roman Empire, sometimes serving as a quarry for those who were too lazy to go and dig out their own building stones from the ground. Even today there is a good deal of the wall left—no longer a grim reminder of the might of the legions, but an ancient monument which seems to fit into the landscape as well as it ever did in the days of the Caesars. There is a deep, and almost "touchable" silence, broken only occasionally by a bird call or the muffled bleating of distant sheep. Even the presence of a handful of tourists fails to disturb the peace overmuch. It was a busier and noisier place in Roman times.

Even when the tribesmen were quiet, it was a rough life on the wall, and one spiced with danger. You put up with this state of affairs if you are a soldier. You know that someone has to get killed in battle, but you never think it will be you! How many foreigners from Jugoslavia or North Africa came to serve the emperor on Hadrian's Wall, little knowing that this was to be the stage on which they acted out their last hours on earth? There are worse places to be buried than amid the folds of the Northumbrian fells at the very edge of the Roman world.

(ii) *THE FORTS OF THE SAXON SHORE*

Rome's history can be fairly divided into three parts: the first was when they were conquering the world as they knew it, the second was when they were trying to sort out and hang on to what they had won and the last was when things began to fall apart. In south east England there is a series of monuments to this third period. A long chain of forts—about a dozen or so—stretches from the north Norfolk coast to Hampshire. Some are impressive ruins, some have been half washed away by the sea, and the very locations of one or two are in doubt. They cover between them about three hundred miles of the English coast nearest to the continent, and they are largely built to control the entrances to harbours and estuaries.

The most northerly one is Branodunum (Brancaster) in Norfolk and the next down the coast is Gariannonum (Burgh Castle) near Great Yarmouth on the Norfolk-Suffolk border. There was possibly a fort at Walton Castle close to Felixstowe but the site has been completely eroded by the sea. Further south are the remains of about half of Othona (Bradwell) on the lonely Essex marshes. Across the Thames in Kent are four more—Regulbium (Reculver), Rutupiae (Richborough), Dubris (Dover) and Lemanis (Lympne). The last two on the list are farther west: they are Anderita (Pevensey) in Sussex and Portus Adurni (Portchester) in Hampshire.

They are built in a slightly different style from earlier Roman works. The walls are higher and even more solid than those of the forts which stood in or along the northern frontier zone. They are protected by round bastions with firing platforms on top of them for the ballistas and catapults—the "guns" of the Roman army. The space inside each fort was big enough to hold detachments of foot soldiers and units of the imperial navy as well. The forts all date from the late third century—some were newly built at that time, whilst others were reconstructed on older foundations.

Modern archaeologists are beginning to reveal a lot of hidden details, but some of the forts, notably those at Portchester, Pevensey, Richborough and Burgh Castle have always been on view. They have set problems for historians throughout the ages, from Bede, the Saxon scholar onward. What exactly were they? Who made them, and why? In earlier years these questions might have been answered like this: "They were built by the Romans to control the Saxons who had already settled in the narrow coastal strip along our southern and eastern shores." Later on, this sort of reply was considered much too vague. Which Romans in particular set them up? And are we so certain that the Saxons had already started to settle in England at this early date?

Because the forts all looked somewhat alike, it was easy to see that they belonged to the same period. More thorough investigation showed that not only was this view correct, but that from a study of the architecture it was possible to say that they had probably been designed by the same man. Who was this man? Historians are agreed that he was either Carausius or Constantius Chlorus. Those who favour the latter say that the system was designed by the emperor to deal with Saxon *raiders*, not Saxon colonists, and it is true that the fierce warriors from the other side of the North Sea were becoming more than just a nuisance at that time.

Those who think Carausius was the man have a more complicated story to tell. Carausius, they say, started his career as an ordinary seaman in the "Classis Britannica", or British Fleet. The fleet's main job was to move the legions and all their gear to wherever they were wanted. This they did very efficiently for more than two hundred years, but at the beginning of Diocletian's reign, pirate ships from north west Europe began to attack the southern and eastern coasts of Britain. So the authorities fitted out a number of war vessels whose task was to drive off the raiders or to capture them. The warships were based at Dover and at Lympne.

Carausius rose rapidly through the ranks, eventually becoming the commander-in-chief of the Classis Britannica. He was extremely good at seizing Saxon long-ships —so good, in fact, that the emperor began to get suspicious, particularly when the loot which he took from the dozens of pirate ships never seemed to get back to its rightful owners. Maximian, who was the emperor's lieutenant (or Caesar, as he had become known) sent spies to Carausius's headquarters in Gaul to find out exactly what was happening.

The reports they sent back were even more startling than the rumours. It seemed that Carausius was not only keeping the booty for himself, he was actually *encouraging* the Saxons to rob merchant ships and coastal towns. The commander-in-chief made sure that he only captured those long-ships which were on their way home. He could therefore be certain that the prize was worth taking. Maximian, now thoroughly alarmed, sent soldiers to arrest Carausius and bring him to trial.

Carausius knew that he would be condemned and executed if he were taken prisoner, so he crossed the Channel to Britain where he had himself proclaimed emperor. Most of the troops accepted him as Augustus, and they managed to beat off an attack hastily thrown together by the emperor Diocletian and his Caesar, Maximian. Realizing that it would take a long time to defeat him, the co-emperors in Rome decided to make the best of a bad job and recognize him as one of themselves. At the same time, they began to make plans to overthrow the usurper.

Carausius himself knew that it was only a matter of some months before the whole might of the Empire was turned against him. Therefore (according to those who support his claim to be the builder of the forts), he set to work to strengthen the defences of Britain and France. So the forts of the Saxon shore must have been built to ward off not Saxon raiders, but the legions of the lawful Roman government.

At last, these legions were ready to attack once more, and in the year 293, the Gaulish parts of Carausius's "empire" were overrun. Before the false emperor could prepare himself and his defences for a siege of Britain, he was murdered. The assassin was Allectus, his second-in-command, who wasted no time in taking his place, even to the extent of getting the troops to swear loyalty to himself as emperor. He didn't live long enough to enjoy his new power. A Roman fleet managed to dodge Allectus's ships in a thick fog. Whilst the usurper's warships were patrolling the Channel, the Roman ships were already disembarking the fresh legions which had been sent to defeat him.

Allectus had rounded up every man he could lay hands on, ruthlessly removing whole garrisons from defence lines and forts in the north. Of course, this was what the Caledonians wanted. As soon as they discovered that Hadrian's Wall was deserted, they swarmed across it as they always did, looting, burning and destroying.

Allectus might just as well have left his makeshift

army where it was, for it was soundly beaten by the regular legions of Constantius Chlorus. Allectus was captured and put to death on the spot. Britannia was re-united with the Roman Empire. Constantius now had to beat off the Saxons, drive out the northern invaders and repair all the damage they had done.

Supporters of the second theory therefore say that the man responsible for the Saxon shore forts must have been Constantius. If this is so, then he must also have built the French forts, which are of the same style and date. But some of the forts in Gaul are not even on the coast, so it is a little difficult to see them being used to drive off Saxon long-ships.

Whatever the truth of the matter, the forts are a dramatic reminder of Roman might, whoever built them. Richborough, in particular, is well worth a visit. The walls still stand in places to a height of twenty-five feet (7·5 metres). In the middle of the site are some huge foundations, shaped like a cross. You might think that they are the remains of St. Augustine's chapel, erected to commemorate the spot where the saint's foot first touched English soil in the year 597. In fact, the visitor can indeed see the ruined chapel if he wishes, but the massive cross-like structure is all that is left of a much older monument. It was raised, apparently, to commemorate the Roman victory over the British, and must have been put up well over five hundred years before the saint ever left Rome.

The size of the base seems to show that it once rose some sixty or seventy feet (fifteen to twenty metres) above the ground. Judging from the bits and pieces unearthed nearby, it must have consisted of inscriptions carved in marble, together with a number of bronze and stone statues. It was stripped of all these ornaments some time in the third century, and the stump was probably used as a watchtower. Whoever took the stump down to ground level must have had more patience than the modern archaeologists who dug tunnels under it to see if it was hollow. They discovered that what was left still measured more than thirty feet (nine metres) from top to bottom, and that their drills would bore holes in the pieces of natural flint rather more easily than in the Roman mortar, which was still more than rock-hard after nearly two thousand years!

Once Rutupiae stood on an island guarding the creek which separated the Isle of Thanet from mainland Kent. But Thanet is an island no more. The sea has long since retreated leaving the fort to brood over a stretch of marshland and water meadow. Not very far away stands a nuclear power station.

What would the Romans have thought?

CHAPTER 15

THE END OF ROMAN RULE

AFTER Carausius and Allectus had been removed, it took the government in Rome some time to drive out the barbarians and restore order. Constantius Chlorus eventually died in Britain, worn out by his frequent battles against the Caledonians. His son, Constantine the Great, who had fought alongside him, was proclaimed emperor at York in 306. The barbarians were held— but only temporarily. From this period onward the whole Empire began to show signs of the cracks which were to break it apart.

Outland tribes, attracted by the rich pickings from the settled Roman areas, and driven on by enemies in their own rear, massed against the frontiers whenever they could. Roman emperors one after the other tried to find ways of dealing with them.

Sometimes, whenever the pressure became too great, the government would allow some of the tribesmen to cross certain of the frontiers. In return for this, the tribal chiefs had to promise to keep out any fresh invaders. This was easy to promise but harder to carry out. And a few chieftains, of course, hadn't the slightest

144

intention of barring the road to their kinsmen. Another cause of breakdown, as we have already seen, was the readiness with which provincial governors left their areas unguarded whenever they thought there was a chance of becoming emperor.

Increasingly, the army had the final decision as to who was to be their next ruler. If they didn't like the man they had chosen, he was murdered and a new candidate selected. Quite a few emperors were unofficially condemned to death because they weren't generous enough with cash rewards to the soldiers who had elevated them. Towards the end of the Empire, the legions were almost the least Roman thing about it. The Romans of Italy had long ago left the art of war to Africans, Spaniards, Rumanians, Dutchmen and anyone else they could get to fight for them. Now at this late hour, the army was even recruiting men who had been born outside the Empire altogether. Their loyalty could not be relied on, or taken for granted—it had to be bought.

We have seen how the wealthiest of the Romano-Britons were called upon to supply the cash needed by the government, and how many of them had left the towns rather than pay the crippling taxes demanded. At first, town life, and then towns themselves began to decay as a result.

Tiles were blown off house roofs by the winds and not replaced. The wooden timbers underneath then began to go rotten. Weeds grew more easily in the streets, now that there weren't so many feet to tread them down. In Verulamium, the theatre had long been disused. Where there had once been fights between gladiators, now there were only stealthy figures creeping over the ruins at night to steal what was worth taking. Later still, in spite of attempts to revive town life, the theatre seems to have been used as a rubbish dump.

The cities were among the finest things which Roman civilization had brought to Britain but they were always rather an artificial creation; they never grew naturally out of the needs of the countryside. Most of them were built because *Rome* had decided that they were essential. They required a great deal of money to keep them running, and money was the one thing the government no longer had. When the emperors of the later Empire began trying to take money out of the towns instead of putting it in, those Britons who were expected to pay went to live in the country where the tax man couldn't get at them. The villas went on flourishing well after the towns had passed their point of no return. The main worry of the villa owners was how to protect them from barbarian attacks during the frequent absences of the garrison troops.

Saxons, Angles and Franks continually raided the southern and eastern coasts, whilst the Britons of Wales and the northwest had to try and defend themselves against parties of Scots who were crossing over from their homes in Ireland at about the same time. All these pirates confined themselves mostly to robbing or plundering villages and towns near the seashore. But the "Picts" (or "Painted Ones"), as the Romans were beginning to call the naked blue savages of the north, went on battering away at Hadrian's Wall until they found the garrison was either absent or at least too weak to stop them. When that happened, everyone trembled, for they ranged far and wide, striking terror into the hearts of those living hundreds of miles to the south.

There were waves of onslaughts and periods of peace. The Romano-Britons breathed sighs of relief whenever there was an emperor in Rome strong enough to halt the attacks and restore law and order. But in the last half of the fourth century, the periods of peace grew shorter and shorter.

Between 364 and 367 there was a combined assault on Britannia by all the barbarian tribes at once. Again the central government drove them off and tried to repair the damage they had done. In spite of all that had occurred, it appeared that Rome had still not learned its lesson. Only a dozen or so years later, another British commander set off for the capital with his legions in order to seize the throne. Once more the road to the south was open to the Picts, who lost no time in taking it. A handful of soldiers on the Wall tried to defend it. According to some historians, they were defeated, not by the Picts, but by treachery. This was the very last time that regular Roman troops were used in an attempt to hold back the Picts. The Wall was never reoccupied.

At the end of the fourth century and at the start of

the fifth, the tribes of barbarians called Vandals and Goths began to invade Italy itself. The chief citizens of Britain appealed to the emperor Honorius in Rome to save them. Honorius was much too busy preparing the defences of the Empire's chief city, and he advised the Britons to save themselves if they could.

There is no reliable evidence one way or the other, but it is just possible that a later emperor did in fact send help. If he did, it was short lived. By the year 429 at the very latest, the central government had finally abandoned Britain to its fate. A second appeal was sent to Rome in 446. We don't know how long the Britons waited for an answer. It must have seemed to many of them that it was only a matter of time before the barbarians were driven out of Italy. Then, they reasoned, the emperor would once again be able to send his legions to combat these fierce, barbaric invaders.

Shadowy, heroic figures such as Arthur probably account for the slow advance of the Saxons. It was perhaps two centuries before the English had settled all over the area which we now call England. But long before that, the most hopeful Briton must have realized that no help could reach them from the capital and that no answer would ever be received from the emperor again.

Roman rule in Britain was at an end.

EPILOGUE

IT HAS been the fashion in recent years to look upon the last days of Roman rule as a sorrowful acceptance by the Britons that the good old days were over. The characters in modern plays about the period all seem to be quite sure that this was the end of civilization—but were they? It is just as likely that Romano-Britons were no more certain that the Empire had finally collapsed, than the men of Henry VII's time were aware that the Middle Ages were over. The Britons kept on asking Rome for help, and for their part, the Romans fully intended to return—some day.

The western half of the Empire was overrun and the legions never came back. While the Vandals and Goths were sacking Rome, the Saxons were arriving here in ever larger numbers. They and their ancestors came to these islands as robbers; when the legions had gone for good, they didn't return home but settled down in England. The rough and ready sailors became rough and ready

farmers. They were no more eager to live in Roman
towns than the Belgae had been, four hundred years
before. The decay of both the towns and the villas was
hastened by the Saxon habit of using them as stone
quarries whenever they wanted to add a new cowshed to
their farms.

Roman roads had been carefully surveyed and en-
gineered; Saxon roads were nothing like that. The
Saxons merely walked from village to village if they
couldn't do the trip by boat. If enough people took the
same journey a path would appear: eventually, with the
passage of cows, sheep and horse-drawn carts, the path
got churned up into a muddy lane. This is not to say
that the Saxons never used the roads they found—of
course they did. But they never repaired them. If a

tree fell across their route, or a blocked drain washed part of the surface away, they simply walked round the obstruction. It is probably true to say that Roman roads were built with hands and the Saxon ones with feet! From this it is easy to see that the Saxons adopted whatever parts of Roman civilization took their fancy and ignored the others.

Not all Britons were killed in battle: some were captured and treated as slaves and some fled westward before the advancing English, as we must now call them. There is an inscription on a window sill at Llanmadoc church in the Gower peninsula of South Wales, dating probably from the sixth century. It shows that the Latin tongue was not completely dead. It reads:

BVECHIHLINS
CƆANHIC IACIT

(Ductus son of Guan lies here)

In spite of evidence like this, it is almost certain that quite a few Britons did not escape to the west, but stayed where they were. After all, a great many place names in the southern and eastern parts of the country are British in origin, not English. It is hard to imagine how rivers and hills could have kept their Celtic names until modern times if all the Britons had either been driven off or killed: someone must have remained to tell the English settlers what they were. Perhaps the slaves did this—or could it be that some of the Britons actually intermarried with the English?

The purely Saxon part of our history lasted half as

long again as the Roman.   Claudius's conquest of Britain
was farther in the past to Harold, last of the Saxon kings,
than he is to us.   It is strange to think of the larger
Roman remains being visible throughout the six hundred
years of Saxon rule. More of the smaller reminders are
being turned up by the archaeologist's trowel month by
month.

The Roman relics which the diggers find usually end
up in museums, and every now and then one of these
relics catches at the imagination.   The article in question
does not need to be made of gold, or indeed to be at all
what we think of as valuable.

A good example of this kind of thing is a tile found
near Newgate in London on which a resentful workman
had scratched, "Austalis dibus XIII vagatur sib cotidim'.
(Austalis has been going off on his own every day for
nearly a fortnight!)   There are also human and animal
footprints in wet clay or concrete.   One example from
St. Albans has already been mentioned on page 107.

It would be a dull archaeologist who did not feel some
sort of historical thrill at digging up a Roman coin, for
instance.   The bronze token might have been last handled
by some Latin-speaking Romano-Briton more than fifteen
hundred years before.   The great triumphal arches of the
Caesars may leave us cold but the occasional personal
possession which the excavator finds can sometimes light
up the Roman world in a way denied to the more "impressive" remains.   A letter from a wealthy young citizen
to his friend, a Roman ladder, a small boy's swimming
trunks, a modern-looking water pump, or an equally up-
to-date carpenter's smoothing plane—the list could go
on a lot longer than this.   But perhaps the thing which
really speaks to us across the years is the simple tombstone inscription.

That the Romano-Britons of the remote past could

experience the same kinds of emotions that we do is shown by the three examples which end this book:

"DIS MANIBUS
ATILIAN(US) ET (?) . .
 N.
IPATILIANUS AN
 (NORUM) IIX
PROTUS AN(NORUM)
 XII
  POMPEIUS
  OPTATUS. DO
  MINUS F.C."

"To the spirits of the departed. Atilianus and — ? Ipatilianus aged 8, Protus aged 12. Erected by Pompeius Optatus, their master"
(Chester)

"D.M. SIMPLICIAE
 FLORENTINE
ANIME
 INNOCENTISSIME
QUE VIXIT MENSES
 DECEM
FELICIUS SIMPLEX
 PATER FECIT
 LEG VI V"

"To Simplicia Florentina. A most innocent soul who lived only ten months. Felicius Simplex (of the 6th legion), her father set it up."
(York)

"JULIA MATER
NA AN(NORUM) VI
 JUL(IUS)
MARCELLINUS
FILLIAE CARISSIMAE"

"Julia Materna. Aged 6. Julius Marcellinus to his dearest daughter."
(Corbridge)

Were these children drowned in a flood, perhaps? Were they killed in a riot or carried off by the plague? We shall never know. All we can be certain of is that these touching memorials will continue to keep fresh the memory of the very human people of the Roman world long after we ourselves are gone.

A SELECTION OF SITES IN ROMAN BRITAIN WITH THEIR LATIN NAMES

Aldborough (Yorks)	Isurium Brigantum
Anglesey	Mona
Bath	Aquae Sulis
Bradwell	Othona
Brough-on-Humber	Petuaria
Buxton	Aquae Arnemetiae
Caerleon	Isca Silurum
Caerwent	Venta Silurum
Caister (Norfolk)	Venta Icenorum
Canterbury	Durovernum Cantiacorum
Carlisle	Luguvallium
Chester	Deva
Chesters	Cilurnum
Chichester	Noviomagus Regnensium
Cirencester	Corinium Dubunnorum
Colchester	Camulodunum
Corbridge	Corstopitum
Dorchester (Dorset)	Durnovaria
Dover	Dubris
Exeter	Isca Dumnoniorum
Gloucester	Glevum
Housesteads	Vercovicium
Leicester	Ratae Coritanorum
Lincoln	Lindum
London	Londinium
Lympne	Lemanis
Pevensey	Anderita
Portchester	Portus Adurni
Reculver	Regulbium
Richborough	Rutupiae
Rochester	Durobrivae

Saint Albans	Verulamium
Silchester	Calleva Atrebatum
Staines	Pontes
Wight (Isle of)	Vectis
Winchester	Venta Belgarum
Wroxeter	Viroconium
York	Eburacum

This is only a short selection of Roman place names. The Ordnance Survey map of Roman Britain lists nearly three hundred of them. It is interesting to see that the Romans very often just altered the original Celtic name so that they could say it more easily, and for the same reason the Saxons then Anglicized the Latin form. To the Saxons, most Roman sites were "camps", so they added the Latin word for a camp or fort to the name which they used. Thus it is nearly always possible to say that a town had a Roman beginning, merely because "cester", "caster" or "chester" appears in the final version. It is frequently sheer laziness that causes a name to change through the centuries. It may seem far-fetched but the word "York" is really a mangled form of "Eburacum". The first part of the word to be dropped was probably the last: "Eburacum" would then become "Eburac" or something like it. If the "b" and the "a" were also to disappear, we would be left with "Eurc". Of course, this is not exactly how it happened but if you try to say "Eurc" you will find that what emerges is not unrecognizable. An easier example is "Vectis". The ending "is", like the "um" of Eburacum was soon discarded, leaving us with "Vect". If you leave the "h" out of "Wight" and pronounce the word with a "v" sound at the beginning, as many Germanic languages do today, the result is very close to the Latin name.

SOME EVENTS IN THE HISTORY OF ROMAN BRITAIN

B.C.

First century	Much of S.E. England settled by the Belgae. Some trade with the Roman Empire via Gaul.
55	Julius Caesar's first expedition.
54	Julius Caesar's second expedition.

A.D.

First century *10–40* (approx.)	Cunobelinus rules at Colchester, and is looked upon as "over-king" by a number of other tribes. At the same time, Cogidubnus becomes friendly with the Romans. The Roman Republic collapses and the reign of the emperors begins.
40	Caligula's "invasion" of Britain that never happened.
43	Claudius's invasion of Britain. Aulus Plautius leads the legions. Claudius arrives just in time for the final assault on Colchester. He stays here only sixteen days.
45–49	Supply base at Fishbourne in use by the Second (Augusta) Legion. Its commander, Vespasian, reduces the hill forts of the west. Roads built in S.E. England and the Fosse Way line set up.
49–50	Building of the colonia at Colchester.
51	Caractacus seeks sanctuary with the Brigantes after his defeat but the queen, Cartimandua, hands him over to the invaders.

61   Anglesey captured.   Boudicca leads the
Iceni in revolt.   Colchester, St. Albans
and London sacked.   She is defeated
near High Cross and takes her own life.
Rebel tribesmen hunted down by Suetonius.   He is replaced by Petronius
Turpilianus and Gaius Julius Alpinus
Classicianus, who gradually pacify the
country.

71–74   Petilius Cerialis, governor, overruns the
territory of the Brigantes in northern
England.   The palaces at Fishbourne
and London are begun.   Legionary
fortress built at York.

74–78   Frontinus conquers most of Wales and
establishes garrisons there.   Legionary
fortresses built at Caerleon and Chester.

78–85   Julius Agricola wins battles against the
Scottish   tribes.   Legionary   fortress
built at Inchtuthill.   Agricola recalled
to Rome before he can complete the
conquest of Scotland and possibly Ireland as well.   Scottish gains are never
really   followed   up—territory   slowly
abandoned during the next few years.

90–96   Colonia at Lincoln begun, followed in
the   next   few   years   by   another   at
Gloucester.   General   development   of
Romanized towns now well under way.
The first years of the second century
see many forts and camps made permanent by rebuilding them in stone.

Second century

121   Hadrian tours round the Empire's defences.   He visits Britain and orders the

building of the wall which bears his name. The work takes six to ten years.

139–143   Urbicus fights against the Scottish tribes. The Antonine Wall is built from the Forth to the Clyde.

155–158   Tribes revolt in the north of England. Romans have to leave the Antonine Wall and fall back on Hadrian's. The Antonine Wall is probably reoccupied but finally given up within the next three or four decades. Development of towns and villas in the peaceful south now reaches its peak.

196–197   Chaos in Rome. Clodius Albinus tries to seize power and leaves for the capital with all his troops. He is defeated and killed by Severus, who becomes the next emperor. But the northern British tribes, encouraged by Clodius's absence, overrun the Wall and capture some forts. Hadrian's Wall is recaptured by the Romans, who repair it and re-build the forts that were destroyed. This takes about ten years. During this period, many towns are given walled defences for the first time.

Third century
208   Severus visits Britain with his two sons, Geta and Caracalla, and wins a number of battles against the barbarian northerners.

211   Severus, worn out by his campaigns, retires to York where he dies.

212   Caracalla murders his brother and

thousands of Geta's supporters. He offers Roman citizenship to all free men throughout the Empire in order to increase his income from taxes. Britain is by now split up into two separate provinces.

225–274 Town life in Britain begins to decline. Emperors not quite so much in control as they had been. More than half of the emperors of this period died violently —a good many of them being murdered—some of them reigning for months or weeks rather than years.

Britain and part of Gaul become "independent", being ruled by anyone strong enough to seize power. Saxon raids begin. Wales and western England raided from Ireland. Roman soldiers are harder to come by, for the barbarians are attacking other frontiers as well.

287 Carausius proclaimed "emperor" of Britain and Gaul. Forts of the Saxon Shore are built. Towards the end of the century the Empire is divided in two (although still under the control of the emperor, Diocletian). Each half is ruled by an "Augustus" with a "Caesar" to help him.

293–4 Constantius, the ruler of the west, wins most of Gaul back from Carausius, who is murdered by Allectus.

296 Allectus defeated by Constantius and killed. Britain is once more back in the Empire. During the troubles, the bar-

barians have again damaged the Wall and some of the forts. Britain divided into four provinces. Attempts are made to revive town life, which is still in decline.

Fourth century
306   Constantius Chlorus and his son, Constantine, campaign in Scotland. The countryside thrives during the reign of Constantius, who dies at York, being succeeded by Constantine (later known as "the Great").

313   Edict of Toleration allows Christians to worship freely. Christian churches probably erected or converted from older buildings with official blessing in Britain. Later on, British bishops are recorded as attending the Council of Arles.

343   Constantine's son, Constans, comes to Britain to fight against the Picts and Scots.

360   Julian becomes emperor and tries to bring back the worship of the old gods. He sends Lupicinus to deal with raiding parties of Picts from Scotland and Scots from Ireland.

364–367   Combined onslaught on Roman Britain by all the barbarians at once. Hadrian's Wall captured and severely damaged. Invasion attempt by the Saxons. Other Roman frontiers under pressure. Town life no longer attractive to Romano-Britons. Buildings fall into disuse and decay. Roman way of life is concentrated more and more in the villas.

369 Theodosius is sent to drive off the remaining barbarians. The breaches in Hadrian's Wall are hurriedly repaired.

383 By this time, the Empire has been divided into two virtually independent halves. Magnus Maximus, the British commander, takes his troops to mainland Europe in order to seize the throne of the western Empire. Hadrian's Wall is defended by regular troops for the last time. They are unsuccessful and the Wall is finally abandoned. Five years later, Magnus is defeated by Theodosius in northern Italy. Towards the end of the fourth century Vandals and Goths attack Italy itself. Stilicho makes a despairing effort to hold this part of the Empire together, but further attacks on the capital by Alaric and his Goths put the whole Roman system in danger. Troops have to be withdrawn from Britain. A number of army leaders try, one after the other, to take over the post of emperor.

Fifth century

406 A man calling himself Constantine III tries to hang on to France and Spain with the help of what troops remain in Britain.

410 The British disown Constantine III and appeal to Honorius, the emperor in Rome. He tells them to look after themselves.

429

By this date, the last traces of Roman administration are gone, although Romano-Britons try to keep things going. The invasions from north west Europe now begin in earnest. Throughout the rest of the fifth century the Saxons push on ever westward. The magnificent towns and villas are abandoned one by one. The superb road system begins to decay. A last appeal for help is made without reply. In spite of stout resistance by British leaders such as the almost legendary Arthur, the Saxons take more and more of the country. By the sixth century, southern Britain has become England.

A SHORT LIST OF BOOKS ON ROMAN BRITAIN

Birley, A.   *Life in Roman Britain*   Batsford
Boon, G.   *Roman Silchester*   Parrish
Brailsford, J.   *Antiquities of Roman Britain*
                                                 Br. Museum
Collingwood & Myres   *Roman Britain & the English Settlements*   Oxford
Cottrell, L.   *The Great Invasion*   Evans
Cottrell, L.   *The Roman Forts of the Saxon Shore*
                                                 H.M.S.O.
Cottrell, L.   *Seeing Roman Britain*   Evans
Dudley & Webster   *The Roman Conquest of Britain*
                                                 Batsford
Liversidge, J.   *Britain in the Roman Empire*
                                   Routledge and Kegan Paul
Margary, I.   *Roman Roads in Britain*   Phoenix
Meates, G.   *Lullingstone Roman Villa*   Heinemann
Merrifield, R.   *Roman City of London*   Benn
Priestley, H.   *Britain Under the Romans*   Warne
Quennell, M. & C.   *Everyday Life in Roman and Anglo-Saxon Times*   Batsford
Richmond, I.   *Roman Britain*   Penguin
Sellman, R.   *Roman Britain*   Methuen
Titterton, A.   *Britain Before the Romans*   Ginn
Titterton, A.   *Roman Soldiers*   Ginn
Titterton, A.   *Roman Towns & Country Houses*   Ginn
Webster, G.   *The Roman Army*
                                   Grosvenor Museum, Chester
Wilson, D.   *Roman Frontiers of Britain*   Heinemann
Roman Britain   B.B.C. Publications

Map of Roman Britain   Ordnance Survey
Map of Hadrian's Wall   Ordnance Survey

This is only a brief selection of books on the subject. Some of the most interesting publications are the pamphlets sold at the sites of the principal Roman remains.

ROMAN SITES TO VISIT IN BRITAIN

Bath. In the city of Bath itself are the impressive remains of a considerable late 1st century bath suite. There are circular, oval and oblong baths still fed by warm subterranean springs of mineral-laden water. The great bath is nearly twenty-five yards (over twenty-two metres) long and ten yards (over nine metres) wide, and the whole complex of buildings is over a hundred yards by seventy (ninety metres by sixty). More of it is being excavated as and when opportunity offers.

The adjoining museum displays a good selection of objects discovered during the excavations. Of particular interest are (i) the inscribed altars, (ii) the tombstones with their inscriptions, (iii) part of the roofing structure, as these are fairly rare, and (iv) the Gorgon's head (which, by the way, looks almost as effective upside down!).

Chedworth. A good example of a country gentleman's villa, complete with two courtyards, two bath suites, hypocausts and mosaics. One bath was the normal "Turkish" type but the other was known to the Romans as a "Laconicum", or Spartan bath.* We should probably use the word "Sauna" to describe it because it resembled a Scandinavian bath. The really tough bather went into a room with a dry atmosphere and a very high temperature, where perspiring might even become painful if he stayed in too long. Immediately he came out, he dived into a pool of cold water, or perhaps rolled in the snow during the winter time.

Bignor. A very large villa with the rooms around an

---

* Mentioned on page 69.

open courtyard. The whole complex with its surrounding wall is more than a hundred yards (metres) wide and nearly two hundred yards (metres) long.

Fishbourne. Already mentioned in the main part of the book, this site is a "must".

Hadrian's Wall. Another "must". A lot of the wall is still standing, and the countryside it runs through is nearly as deserted now as it was then. It ran from Bowness, west of Carlisle, to Wallsend, near Newcastle, a distance of 73 miles (117 kilometres). It had numerous forts, turrets, castles and legionary bases, all connected by a military road. Visitors should take time to see:

(i) Corbridge Roman station with its ventilated granaries, the odds and ends of military occupation and the paymaster's underground strongroom.

(ii) Housesteads Fort, which is reached by a stiffish scramble from the car park. It was one of the forts of the auxiliary soldiers who manned the Wall, and later on, the local customs posts. One curiosity is the water tank which still bears the marks of the legionary swords which were apparently sharpened on it. The visitor can climb up on the wall which forms the north face of the fort and trace Hadrian's handiwork striding away over the fells.

(iii) Chesters Roman Fort which was once garrisoned by a crack Spanish cavalry outfit. The military baths were of the finest quality. The fort itself is built on both sides of the Wall so that horsemen could ride out to the north in order to deal with attackers. Nearby are the remains of a Roman bridge over the North Tyne.

St. Albans. A good site museum containing a large model of the town's layout as it was in those days and

a fine model of a city gateway. Some of the fairly uncommon stretches of interior decoration are also to be
found here. The story of how these fragments came to
be rescued from their face-down position and lovingly
prepared for exhibition is worth going into. Visitors
should see the separately preserved hypocaust, the remains of the town walls and the magnificent theatre with
its nearby shop and house foundations.

Silchester. One of the few Roman town sites which has
remained uncovered by later building. It is rather difficult to get to, but well worth a visit. The shape of the
town is defined by the lines of the walls, some stretches
of which are still standing. There is a small museum,
but perhaps the most curious sight, and one which only
shows itself towards the end of a hot, dry summer, is
the reappearance of the town's street plan, marked out
in lines of brown and withered grass amid the surrounding greenery.

Chester. Apart from the usual quota of Roman town
wall fragments, mosaic pavements and similar remains
(the "Roman Gardens"), Chester probably has one of
the finest Roman museums in the country. Among the
exhibits not to be missed are the detailed model of
Roman Chester and a very realistic, full-sized model of
a legionary soldier. The town's amphitheatre is being
excavated and may, perhaps, be opened to the public.
In common with some other Roman settlements, Chester
still keeps part of the original Roman layout in its modern
street pattern.

London. The capital city preserves a surprising amount
of the old city wall with its Roman foundations. Many
of these stretches can be seen from nearby streets, but

some of the most interesting parts are on private property
and can only be viewed by appointment.   Most of
London's general museums have some Roman material
but the two best are the Guildhall Museum and the
recently rearranged British Museum exhibition.   A few
of the round turrets added to the wall in later years
remain standing and can be inspected.   There is one
beneath the courtyard of the G.P.O.'s Mount Pleasant
sorting office.   The temple of Mithras which was excavated in 1954 has been re-erected near the Mansion
House: the visible foundations are alongside the pavement, so no great detour is needed to have a look at it.
Near the Tower of London, in Trinity Place, is a reproduction of the Classicianus monument, the original of
which is in the British Museum.   Also in this museum
is a fine display of a Roman silver dinner service unearthed at Mildenhall in Suffolk.

York.   There are pieces of the Roman town walls together with some of the towers.   There is also an interesting museum containing many personal possessions of
Eburacum's Romano-British inhabitants.   For instance,
there are some children's toys, the sight of which might
serve to remind us that Romans were not merely grim-
faced soldiers in armour, but fathers, husbands and sons
as well.   A length of road on nearby Wheeldale Moor
is paved with some of the original Roman stones.   A
detour to Aldborough, the regional capital of the
Romanized Brigantes, is worthwhile.

Wroxeter.   Quite a lot of Roman Wroxeter is left; for
instance, the bases of the columns which formed one of
the colonnades of the forum are still in position.   But
the most eye-catching thing is the imposing entrance
from the exercise hall to the frigidarium of the corporation baths.   This must be one of the largest and tallest

pieces of non-military Roman wall still standing in Britain. The museum contains, among other things, an inscribed stone which was set up over the main entrance to the forum. The lettering shows that it was dedicated to the emperor Hadrian by the people of the town.

Of course, this is only a short list of the Roman sites in Britain which are worth visiting. Other Roman towns such as Lincoln, Colchester, Cirencester, Chichester, Leicester and Canterbury could have been included. There are dozens of villas to search out, and reminders of the Roman occupation are to be found in the unlikeliest places. The Roman ballista bolt wedged into the spine of a defender of Maiden Castle has already been mentioned—and who would imagine before he was told that there is an almost complete Roman lighthouse in the grounds of the Norman castle at Dover? Richborough, Caerleon, Wall, Caerwent, Portchester, Lullingstone—the tally could be extended much further.

Holiday makers at Folkestone can not only go and see the Roman lighthouse in nearby Dover, they have a villa of their own to explore. Summer visitors to Lowestoft or Great Yarmouth might like to give the beach a miss just for one day so that they can make an excursion to Burgh Castle, that lonely remnant of the Forts of the Saxon Shore, standing amid the fields of cabbage and sugar beet.

In Britain, particularly in the settled south east and in the frontier zones, you are never very far away from some considerable reminder of the Romans. The best way to find out exactly how far is to buy the Ordnance Survey's remarkably good map of Roman Britain, which has references, not only to the principal sites and remains, but also to almost every Roman object of importance ever unearthed.

ACKNOWLEDGEMENTS

The author wishes to thank the following people for their invaluable assistance in the gathering of material about the unearthing of the Roman palace at Fishbourne for this book:

Mr A. N. Burgess and Mr P. M. Harvey, both of the City of Portsmouth Water Company;
Mrs Margaret Rule and Mr Barry Cunliffe, archaeologists;
Mrs Peggy Anderson, a local resident interested in the past of her neighbourhood;
The Sunday Times.

The publishers wish to thank the following for their kind permission to reproduce their photographs:
The Radio Times Hulton Picture Library for "A Roman road, Wheeldale Moor, Yorkshire"; "Hadrian's Wall near Housesteads Fort"; "Portchester Castle, a Saxon Shore fort"; "Roman pins, spoon, probe, spatula and stilus (pen)"; and "Roman kitchenware—saucepan, ladle, plate and cake tin".
Popperfoto for "Roman villa at Chedworth, Gloucestershire, as it is today"; "Archaeologists discover the temple of Mithras in London"; and "Remains of Housesteads Fort, Hadrian's Wall".
The Mansell Collection for "Reconstruction of the Chedworth villa"; and "Roman shoes and sandals found in London".
The trustees of the London Museum for "Reconstruction of Roman London".
The Guildhall Museum for "A wooden writing tablet and stiluses (pens)".

INDEX

172

176 INDEX